S0-BCT-666

Heroes
and
Humanities

WITHDRAWN

WITHDRAWN

Heroes
and
Humanities

Detective Fiction
and
Culture

Ray B. Browne

1986

141 pp.

Bowling Green State University Popular Press
Bowling Green, Ohio 43403

Acknowledgements

Three of these essays have appeared in *Clues: A Journal of Detection*. "Sherlock Holmes as Christian Detective: *The Case of the Invisible Thief*," *Clues* 4:1 (Spring/Summer 1983), pp. 79-92; "The Heroic World of Judson Philips," *Clues* 6:1 (Spring/Summer 1985), pp. 79-96; "The Frontier Heroism of Arthur W. Upfield," *Clues* 7:1 (Spring/Summer 1986) pp. 127-145.

My thanks to the Editor, Pat Browne, for permission to reprint these essays, somewhat altered.

Copyright ©1986 by Bowling Green State University Popular Press

Library of Congress Catalogue Card No.: 86-72643

ISBN: 0-87972-370-X Clothbound
0-87972-371-8 Paperback

For Pat
My Enthusiastic Co-conspirator

CONTENTS

Introduction

Mystery fiction although essentially the same in all its national varieties nevertheless comes in several types and several wrappings. To a certain extent the contents of the packages remain virtually the same but the aims change and the purposes are increasingly more deeply intended and understood.

Historically, of course, the most influential type of mystery fiction has been the British Golden Age, or Classical, or locked-door type, in which a crime, usually a murder, is committed despite the fact that access to the victim is difficult and escape from the scene of the crime virtually denied since no trace of exit has been left. The means of exit therefore is baffling and of great importance. In this type of story the society surrounding the victim is disrupted. The point of the story is to find the guilty person, bring his or her guilt to light, and in so doing restore the equilibrium and security of society.

There are various theories about why such a story is enjoyable. Everybody, of course, loves a story, and everybody loves even more a story that creates suspense and thrills, especially if in the process the reader meets interesting people, particularly detectives and private investigators and their helpers with whom the reader is familiar and with whom the reader can identify. These people constitute bastions of strength on which the reader can rely and depend. Undoubtedly psychologists are correct in attributing to this whole psychological experience some primal urge to solve some of the basic causes of personal and societal insecurity and anxiety. Detective fiction becomes a marsupial's pouch in which adults can climb to escape the fears and troubles which beset them in the world.

Two outstanding examples of this type of fiction are A. Conan Doyle's Sherlock Holmes stories and Agatha Christie's accounts of her several detectives, the most famous of whom is Hercule Poirot. The lasting quality of these investigators is fascinating. They have become so much a part of our culture that we accept them as readily as we do characters from Classical literature and other heroes. Holmes is so popular these days that Holmesiana has spawned a whole cult concerned with every aspect of his and his family's career. Agatha Christie is still the most widely read detective fiction author in the world.

In contrast to the British Golden Age detective fiction, the essentially American so-called "hard-boiled" type approaches the general mystery genre from a notably different point of view. This type involves hard knocks, hard feelings, hard language, a good deal of misogyny. It is usually played out on the "mean streets" of America.

Unfortunately the canon of this so-called "hard-boiled" fiction, as is often the case in popular fiction, has been greatly misunderstood or insufficiently comprehended. It is glib generalization to call this fiction "hard-boiled," which it is in style only. Otherwise it is something else at least in philosophy and motivation.

Generally, of course, all the types of such thriller fiction fit the criteria for detective fiction. There is a crime of some sort, there is a "hero" who sets out to find the perpetrator, and eventually the case is solved. In the process a great deal of physical violence is employed, rough language is used, females are often abused, and there seems to be a great deal of anti-social behavior evidenced. But overriding all the hard

2

aspects of the society and the conduct of the hero is the fact that the physical and psychological profile of the hero indicates not so much his being "hard-boiled" as his being soft-hearted.

In British mystery fiction the hero works for pay, because he is a part of the official police force or a private investigator; sometimes he or she works merely for gentlemanly or ladyly fun. He or she seldom seems to be concerned with the fact that a crime has been committed contrary to law and decency, and the guilty person should be brought to the bar.

In American mystery fiction, on the contrary, the rules of society seem ever before the eyes of the person interested in solving the crime. Generally he or she works for some official agency or is a set of eyes for hire, that is, charges so much a day, plus expenses, for his or her services. But—and this is very important in establishing the true definition of the American genre—if the victim of the crime has no money, American investigators will work for nothing: not for sex or money—for nothing, just because society needs the work and the injured party needs the satisfaction of seeing that "justice" is done. Compassion, the sense of decency, community bonding, the sense of equality before the law and events of life—some human bond drives the investigator to contribute his or her time in bringing the perpetrator of a crime to justice. The investigator may say he has no sense of justice, he might want to be a private avenger of injustice, he may say he has contempt for the law and order he represents. But he works for it nevertheless. It is this American sense of community, of helping one's neighbors—or perpetuating the American Dream—that makes the "hard-boiled" thriller fiction more properly called the "soft-hearted." It is the sense of the American West brought into an urban setting with the need to solve the consequent social and

3

human problems that drives this type of fiction.

In many ways it is the sense that the crimes are affronts to the American Dream that demonstrates how socially conscious this type of fiction is. Hammett's and Chandler's private eyes react to the dirtying of the California landscape by the vicious characters; they want to clean it up. John D. MacDonald's Travis McGee works for pay or for nothing against the giant machines in his society that make pawns of the little and defenseless people. Ross Macdonald's Lew Archer is filled with compassion for the weak, especially children and women, because he knows how hard society grinds people between its iron fists of technology and power. Macdonald deliberately chose southern California as the background of his stories because he felt that in that spot the pressures of life had caught up with the people because with their backs to the sea and unable to run any farther they had to confront the forces that seemed set to destroy them.

American suspense fiction differs in yet another, very significant, way from its British counterpart. British suspense fiction tends to be static in its point of view, changing only in locale and method of developing the commonly accepted role. Thus for this school of fiction John Cawelti's comments on the constrictions of formula are essentially correct when in *Adventure, Mystery and Romance* he says:

Because of the basic intellectual demands it makes on its audience, the pure mystery has become one of the most sophisticated and explicitly artful of formulaic types. Yet its limitations are also great. While the classical detective story was a preeminent type of formulaic literature between the end of the nineteenth-century and the time of World War II, and still remains an important formula, it has not shown the same capacity for change and development as the other major formulaic types. It is possible that the heyday of the pure mystery is past. And yet, as an important element in other formulaic types, mystery will undoubtedly continue to be a basic formulaic resource.

American detective fiction, on the contrary, does not fit Cawelti's generalizations. It is dynamic and developing. Having outgrown the mere investigation of crime, this detective fiction has broken the formula of genre boundaries and has become fiction of crime and punishment in a much larger sense, in other social documents and investigations that transcend the narrowly restrictive and prescribed rules of suspense fiction. Many American writers are interested in the society, the sociology, anthropology, psychology, the total picture of the acts against society. They have become in the broadest sense of the word interested in the humanities—those elements which motivate, inform, control and juvenate our lives. American detective thrillers imitate heroic fiction of all types in making social and philosophical statements about our lives and ways of living, of our society and our world.

The present study of American (and Australian and Canadian) detective fiction concerns literature which speaks in the ways of heroes and humanities about the human condition. All authors studied here, to one degree or another, demonstrate their concern with human society, some more strongly than others, but all with their eyes on the human situation and human existence. At times these studies tilt toward the tragic in their outlook and development. In all instances they center on the humanistic.

In this book I have deliberately avoided those giants of American suspense fiction—such as Hammett and Chandler, the two Macdonalds, Rex Stout, Robert Parker, and scores of others. Instead I have been concerned with a rather carefully chosen group whose works so far, for one reason or another, have been pretty well overlooked and neglected.

Yet they are writers of significant importance. Arthur Upfield, for example, is an author who towers above nearly all other writers of detective fiction. His Detective-Inspector Napoleon Bonaparte—called Bony—is one of the two or three most imaginatively conceived and appealing detectives in the literature of all countries. Certain of the others, though not so powerful in their presentations, center very admirably on the question of the hero and the humanities. Ed Lacy and E.V. Cunningham, for example, address those concerns very effectively. Others, like John Ball, represent a firm and competent hand in the development of a personal style of writing and philosophy-developing. Certain others, Martha Grimes and Martha G. Webb, for instance, demonstrate how competently the detective suspense novel is crafted in the hands of the ever-growing body of American female writers. Their accomplishments are significant, their potential even greater. Hugh Pentecost, under his various names, represents an author who though he is one of the most prolific in American authors of all time undoubtedly has not come in for his full share of appreciative criticism; this essay is an effort to correct that injustice. George C. Chesbro, though his output in detective fiction is somewhat limited, represents a strength in authorship that reminds one of writers in other genres.

Four authors studied here represent "regionalism" in detective fiction at its very strongest. Few if any authors have done a more splendid job in the genre than Thomas B. Dewey. His is Chicago detective fiction at its very best, with his main protagonist named simply "Mac." Indianapolis—and Indiana—detective fiction is splendidly presented in the works of Michael Z. Lewin. He writes with a sense of humor and detachment which is completely satisfying to the casual reader as well as to the one who is looking for messages and philosophy. Lewin is one of the finest writers in the canon. So is Jonathan Valin in his study of the twisted minds and streets of Cincinnati and its environs. The city rises into animated three dimensions under his careful mind and pen. The Mid-west again comes alive in the religious detective fiction of Ralph McInerny, whose keen wit and gentle disposition make his work superior to that of most others in the religious sub-genre.

In Peter Corris we come across a writer who is powerfully Australian in subject matter but international in treatment. In three Canadian writers we find at least one who is keenly concerned with the question of the intermeshing of Canadian-U.S. societies and with the border that separates yet joins both. Finally, in the very strange book *The Case of the Invisible Thief*, by Thomas Brace Haughey, we get a study in religious detective fiction that perhaps should have succeeded but apparently failed. Perhaps the hard-rocks of skepticism in our society does not provide enough soil for the growth of such fiction. Maybe it is better left undeveloped, but it surely provides an interesting glance into a part of American culture that is today becoming more and more apparent if not important.

Whether or not these books flourish in their time, they and their authors all represent, to one degree or another, the writers' concern with the hero and his/her role in the humanities. These two aspects of our society provide the common thread which placed these books in this study and which hold my book together. The field continues to be one that interests and concerns many readers, not only for the skill with which the authors work but also for the importance of the subject matter they all address. They—and this kind of detective fiction—deserve more attention.

The Frontier Heroism of Arthur W. Upfield

The essence of frontier heroic literature commits a hero against evil forces in a setting where nature is powerful and is either indifferent or hostile and therefore presents awesome difficulties for the hero. In this setting, the superperson fights for the good of individuals and of society as a whole. Part of the accomplishment of the hero is in triumphing over or in the presence of powerful nature which if not hostile seems to be purposefully throwing obstacles in the path of the hero in his quest.

Since part of the heroic stature of the individual comes from overcoming the forces raised by nature, he becomes a *natural* hero as opposed to a *social* hero that arises as society becomes more the battleground. The forces of nature extend beyond mere earthly setting, of course, and rise to the supernatural in the shape of evil or indifferent gods who may or may not be interested in the fate of man.

Two classic American writers who perhaps most clearly exemplify these two aspects of the hero are James Fenimore Cooper in the Leatherstocking Tales, in the person of Natty Bumppo (in his various names), and Herman Melville in at least a half dozen characters, the most notable of whom are Ahab in *Moby-Dick* and Billy Budd in the short novel of the same name.

Bumppo combats evil Indians and treacherous whites for the benefit of individuals and through them society. But his battles are waged in the presence of a second powerful force, nature, which although at times benign or indifferent, nevertheless constitutes a force that often becomes hostile and must always be reckoned with.

In Melville the frontier is of a slightly different kind: it is a transcendental nature sometimes embued with a supernatural spirit which seems to combat the godliness in mankind. When Melville's heroes struggle for themselves and mankind they must fight on at least two levels and sometimes against three foes: man, nature and God. Thus on two levels the battles of these two authors exemplify the essence of the heroic, frontier struggle. The authors are concerned with the hero in epical battles.

Arthur W. Upfield (1888-1964), one of two or three of the major Australian popular authors, resembles Cooper and Melville perhaps more than he does any other authors. His settings are similar. His working area is the whole of the continent of Australia, as Cooper's were the whole frontier and Melville's the entire frontier of Transcendentalism. Upfield's antagonists are nature and man, and in Australia, nature, often more terrible than man, is always heroic. Upfield's protagonist is Detective-Inspector Napoleon Bonaparte—called Bony by himself, his friends in the books, and by his readers. He faces deserts of sand hundreds of miles across, sand spouts fifty miles wide, rabbits in the millions, lakes that dry up in water spouts that blot out the sun, great distances of miles and the loneliness that comes in such a country. "Common to all" says Upfield in *Man of Two Tribes* "is the force of opposition to man." The country, he adds, "will destroy any man who goes out alone." This is perhaps Upfield's reason for trying to discover and instill compassion and communality among his people.

But Upfield's fiction differs somewhat from that of Cooper and Melville. Whereas theirs is epical, and therefore concerned with a nation and a people, Upfield's is crime fiction, therefore concerned with crime and punishment, though against a background of civilization against pre-civilization.

Nearly all detective fiction develops through heroes and heroines as protagonists. Generally these heroes combat crime to set society aright after the intrusion of a convulsion of crime that has knocked it askew, to piece together the elements of a puzzle or to protect society. Such heroes are *social* heroes. Upfield's hero is different. His books are about frontier offenses and retribution. They are conventional books in that the hero is a superman of sorts, with the classic birth which is mysterious and somewhat unusual. In *Man of Two Tribes* (p. 2) Bony gives perhaps the most succinct description of his origin: "I never knew my father.... I never knew my mother either. She was found dead under a sandalwood tree, with me on her breast and three days old.... In spite of my parentage, I am unusual. Or is it because of my parentage?" Bony readily and frequently admits that there is no crime he cannot solve.

In many ways Bony is also "godlike." He prefers crimes that are somewhat old. Time, as he says, is an ally. He does not like to witness violence; and Upfield does not portray much crime on stage. Most of his is done offstage or was committed in the past. Bony does not particularly care whether criminals are punished for their crimes. He likes to solve crimes because they provide him with mental exercise, and in that respect he is a standard cerebral detective, and having solved them he at least once acts as judge and dismisses the criminal, wishing the guilty person a happy future.

The world in which Upfield works is different from that of other detective writers. It is different from America in being a society that is less generally violent though just as down-to-earth and realistic. Upfield is more deeply and more directly concerned with the physical and natural background than other detective fiction authors who write about other continents: any of the English, George Simenon about France, Wahloo and Sjowall and their stories about Sweden, H. R. F. Keating and his stories about India; Robert Van Gulik and his tales about Judge Dee in Classical China; and Elspeth Huxley and James McClure and their probing stories of crime in Africa. These people are more concerned in the conventional way with people and social justice. In other words, these are books about *social* crime. Upfield's are different.

Upfield's books are perhaps the most heroic of Australian popular writings. Whereas other popular writers like Colleen MacCullough in *The Thornbirds* and Nevil Shute in *A Town Called Alice* are epical and therefore heroic in their presentations of life in Australia, Upfield writes of substantially the same kind of subject but with less epical sweep. He is more concerned with the narrowly heroic aspect, though he writes of virtually every aspect of Australian life of the first half of the twentieth century: the outback, cattle and sheep raising, drought, combatting "vermin" (rabbits), crime in small cities, mining, the sea, etc.

Upfield is similar to Cooper and Melville, especially Melville, in that he was not college trained. As Melville declared that the whaleship was his Harvard and Yale (and reacted against his lack of formal education though he was widely read in his own way), Upfield, who was born in England and sent by his father to Australia because there he would be least nuisance to his parents in England, said that the continent of Australia was his Oxford and Cambridge. Like Melville in his own world, Upfield wandered the Continent, doing every kind of manual labor available, thereby gaining firsthand knowledge of the world he would later write about. Like Melville, also, Upfield became a voracious and wide reader.

Unlike Melville, however, Upfield made his hero a college graduate (M.A. Brisbane University) with the social graces that would enable him to ingratiate himself into the most polite society, yet with the naturalness that would allow him to move in the meanest society. In fact, the tension that arises in the conflict between the two societies drives Bony's attitude and action. Bony—Everyman in the sense of Billy Budd and Ishmael— was the great hero-equalizer between the two societies and between the two races, the white and the aborigines.

Bony is like Cooper's Natty Bumppo in being caught between two worlds. He is a half-breed, his mother having been an aborigine, his father an Englishman. This dual nature, which Melville in *Moby-Dick* said is the ideal mixture of races, gave Bony the best of both cultures: the reasoning nature of his father and the warm-hearted intuition of the aborigine which allowed him to follow invisible trails through sand and over rocks that no white and few pure abos could follow. The character of Bony (which was based on a man named Tracker Leon whom Upfield met in his travels throughout Australia) allowed Upfield to study the situation of the two cultures in Australia to point out the characteristics and to make his suggestions for a solution to the problems.

On the subject Upfield wrote thirty-three books (Bony is in 29 of them) and numerous short stories (some of which are not available in the United States, though the canon is being republished in two or three places now). Some of the subjects are narrow, almost ordinary detection and conventional accomplishments, though they present little-known and interesting aspects of Australian life. All have moments that could have been created only when the subject is Australian life and the author Arthur Upfield, and the detective the fascinating Bony, whom all readers classify as among the most successful half dozen detectives of all crime fiction. At his best, moreover, Upfield in his concept of Bony and the challenge of detective fiction against nature and man, and the power of his accomplishment in working out the story can be compared with the absolute strongest.

Upfield makes it clear from the beginning of his series that Bony walks between two cultures, at times blessed by his mixed blood, at times cursed:

He walked with the soft tread of the Australian aboriginal. Of medium height and in his early to middle forties, free from impeding flesh, and hard as nails, there was yet in his carriage more of the white man than of the black. By birth he was a composite of the two. His mother had given him the spirit of nomadism, the eyesight of her race, the passion for hunting; from his father he had inherited in overwhelming measure the white man's calm and comprehensive reasoning: but whence came his consuming passion for study was a mystery.

Bony, as he insisted on being called, was the citadel within which warred the native Australian and the pioneering, thrusting Britisher. He could not resist the compelling urge of the *wanderlust* any more than he could resist studying a philosophical treatise, a revealing autobiography, or a ponderous history. He was a modern product of the limitless bush, perhaps a little superior to the general run of men in that in him were combined most of the virtues of both races and extraordinarily few of the vices. (*Winds of Sandee*, 1931, pp. 1-2).

In almost every book Upfield makes his point clear. In Bony the two races—the primitive and the civilized, the past and the present—struggle. Caught in the crossfire of the two civilizations, Bony, led by his heart, almost has to become a cultural conservative, though he is never quite sure where he stands. He benefits personally from the mixture, as does his half-breed wife and half-breed children; he is always proud of his station in life and invariably leaves the bush and the aborigines to return to his cultured home. But Bony has not departed far from his upbringing. His civilization "was but a veneer laid upon the ego of modern man" and he was "often [a] tragic figure, in whom ever warred the influence of two races" (*The Mountains Have a Secret*, 1952, p. 93). At times in reaction to some monstrous act by whites he would declare, "It was full time that the Creator of man wiped out altogether this monster called civilization and began again with the aborigines as a nucleus" (*The Bone is Pointed*, 1938, p. 121).

But generally Upfield is not content with such a conclusion. His books approach the subject from varying points of view. In the most extremely folkloristic and anthropological of his books, *The Bone is Pointed*, Upfield has Bony tracing out a small group of aboriginals who have for their own purposes committed a murder. Bony, who intellectually is pure white, is nevertheless caught up in the voodoo of the black rituals, and when the bone is pointed at him (the curse laid on him), he becomes sick and almost dies, his nature telling him he cannot resist, his subconscious driving him to fight the curse.

He overcomes the pointed bone, solves the murder and though there has obviously been a tug of war in his nature over the importance of the aboriginal culture and that of the whites, the latter triumphs in Bony's nature. At the end of the book he heads for the city in the strongest symbol of white man's progress that he could have used, an airplane, and he heads into the sunset and toward civilization where reason searches for truth in a kind of apotheosis: "The scarlet mist and the scarlet sun painted the machine with glowing colour,and made scarlet searchlights of its windows" (*The Bone is Pointed*, p. 288).

Sometimes Upfield's working out the conflict between the two cultures is Romantic in the historical sense of the word. One book, *Bony and the Black Virgin* (1959), is Hemingwayesque in its starkness, love, use of nature and in its denouement. It is a stark rendition of what happens in Australia when East meets West, that is when white meets aborigine in a setting in which the two are not and cannot be equals: A white man grows up with a beautiful aborigine child and they mature into a love for each other which comes natural and overrides all other considerations. Yet the white man's family will not accept the black lady as their equal, and the aboriginal society will not accept the white man into their tribe. The situation presents a problem that even Upfield does not quite know how to handle. Bony's heart lies with the aboriginals: "So many people fail to see these aborigines for what they are. To regard them as uncouth savages is such a boost for the ego, and yet, search as you might, you won't find a moron among them. I know an aboriginal head man who might have skipped four thousand years to come down to this age, for mankind has deteriorated mentally and spiritually" (p. 151). Yet he felt that for the abos "complete assimilation isn't achieved by the aborigine via swift passage from one state to another, as the foreign national is granted citizen rights at a Town Hall ceremony. Assimilation is gradual, and requires several generations" (p. 144).

At the end, Upfield gives in to his conservatism and pessimism and has the book end in a self-destruction that is worthy of Hemingway—shaded a little perhaps by the O'Henry of such a story as "Gift of the Magi." He has the two lovers sail a boat out into a lake and sink it and themselves.

Of all authors who write about heroes, Upfield at his strongest reminds us of Herman Melville at his most powerful, when he is writing of the essence of the hero. Upfield accomplishes this parallel in at least three ways: 1) in his notion of the brotherhood of all men and women; 2) in his rhetoric and 3) in his symbolism.

Upfield is one of the most humanistic of authors. In writing about the great schism and conflict between the aborigines and the whites, he develops in dozens of places the aspects of life that they have in common and the need for each to respect the rights and culture of the other so that they can come together in the end. Though he realizes that there is a cultural lag in the civilization of the abos, he insists that in some ways they are superior to the whites who condescend to them. As Melville insisted in his way, Upfield echoes that all people belong to the great League of Nations, and as such they need to be treated with respect (*The Bone is Pointed*, p. 166).

In many ways Upfield approaches Melville in his figures of speech. Both authors thought of nature as a symbol, both conceived cosmically and both were powered by great outbursts of rhetorical flourish. Upfield sounds Melvillian, for example, in one passage where he addresses and describes nature: "Old Man Drought was dead, battered and bludgeoned by the drops of water. The beaten Earth, ravished and scared, bedraggled and weary, conceived, and the womb prepared to give forth its fruit" (*Bony and the Black Virgin*, p. 121). To Upfield Nature is a Bible: "The print of the Book of the Bush doesn't quickly vanish" (*Virgin*, p. 178). He repeats this concept in one way or another in virtually every book. Sometimes the acts of nature are demonic: "Like a thousand devils the wind howled among the trees and plucked at their branches to tear them away from the parent trunks and lay them violently on the ground." Sometimes Australian nature creates sand storms that are virtual solid walls of sand swirling up for a circumference of fifty miles (*Wings Above the Diamantina*, p. 105). Upfield personifies inanimate things: "The dominating mountain watched. One could not get away from those grey-and-brown eyes. Even in the dense scrub they sought one out" (*The Mountains Have a Secret*, 1952, p. 43)

Sometimes the books begin with an epical sweep and flourish that echoes the cosmos and eternity. In speaking of a set of mountains (in *Mountains*, p. 5), Upfield writes: "They rose from the vast plain of golden grass; in the beginning, isolated rocks along the north-west horizon, rising to cut sharply into the cobalt sky, the rocks united and upon that quarter of the plain it could be seen that a cosmic hurricane had lashed the earth and created a sea, a sea of blue-black waves poised to crash forward in geographical suds."

Sometimes the metaphors and similes surge with heroic gusto: "Another week was devoured by the Year...." (*Death of a Lake*,1954, p. 61). An observer "watched the night extinguish the furnace colours" of a lake (p. 69). Bony saw pelicans "gathered in close-packed mobs like crowds about road accidents" (p. 69). Bony hears a "conversation of water birds." A man (*Murder Down Under*, 1937, p. 298) has "a halo of grey hair resting on his ears."

At times Upfield peoples his stories with characters and humor reminiscent of a mixture of Melville and Dickens.

Almost all the books have characters with funny, descriptive names: Bill the Better is a person who will bet on anything, even against himself (*The Bone is Pointed*). The "Spirit of Australia" is an 80 year old floater who embodies the very essence of the Continent

(*Murder Down Under,* 1937, p. 50). Old Simpson (in *The Mountains Have a Secret,* 1952) is a *Moby-Dick* character: talkative, oracular, wise and experienced. Mr. Penwarden (*The New Shoe,* 1951, p. 166) "looks like Father Time, and the rule he waved in his left hand the scythe." Dead March Harry (in *Deadman's Bend,* 1963, p. 122) is a mental defective who thinks he's dead.

The broadest and most effective comes from *The New Shoe,* where Mr. Penwarden, an old artisan, builds coffins for the people around him. The purchasers try them out before their final use just to make sure that they are comfortable. Mr. Penwarden philosophizes: "Life is a Forge. Sorrow is the Fire and Pain the Hammer. Comes Death to cool the Vessel."

He coaxes Bony to lie down in a coffin to test it and says: "You'd fit nicely. Take off your shoes...might scratch." Bony replies: "I couldn't be more comfortable in bed." On another occasion, Penwarden tells Bony:

"I'll tell'e what...sir.... There is no one now wantin' a first-class coffin, and as'ou just tole me, I must keep me hand in or go sort of stale on the junk. What about one for you, now? A good one to keep out the cold and wet for two or three hundred years?" On another occasion, Penwarden says to Bony: "We all want a corrector...sir, and there's nothin' like the sight of a coffin to melt away pride and vanity."

Two of Upfield's strongest novels are *Mr. Jelly's Business* (1937) and *Bony and the White Savage* (1961). The former is an excellent story of a small town that is caught up in a murder mystery and in solving it Bony's language is stark, idiomatic and powerful.

Bony and the White Savage is the more powerful of the two. It concerns the return of a giant man from prison who had been committed for numerous cases of assault, rape and various other crimes. He is a "psychopath as well as a paranoic" a "gorilla" and a "throwback to a prehistoric monster" yet the people in the small community where he was born and reared looked upon him as an intellectual and good-boy. The point of the novel is the need to educate the naive, to bring them out of their Alice in Wonderland state of mind and get them to recognize evil, which the man is. In doing this, Upfield elevates Marvin, the criminal, into gigantic proportions by frequent references to classical allusions, such as the Trojan horse, to "Bellephon on the back of Pegasus." He illustrates the innocence and naivete of the town by discussing the books they buy and read, such "good blood-and-gutzers" as *Wuthering Heights! Kidnapped! Peyton Place! Blood on the Sand!* and *Ivanhoe,* "a lovely tale."

The style of writing in this book is unusually hard, stark, harsh, and yet at the same time metaphoric and heroic, as witness this one bit of description: "The eye of the wind, having circled toward the Anarctic, had worked on the sea with spectacular results. The Front Door of Australia was now being savaged by all the white ghosts from the South, tearing at the feet of this monolith, leaping high as though to clutch the hair of a giant and pull him down for the lesser attackers to devour" (p. 211).

Upfield's strongest books, in fact, have to do with various aspects of the supernatural. In one book (*Bushranger of the Skies,* 1940), the symbol is an airplane, a common aspect of Australian bush life, and widely used in Upfield's books though never before or after as such a supernatural agent. The symbol in this book is strong, the development powerful, though the book is not necessarily one of Upfield's half dozen most effective books.

In this book the airplane is a demonic agent, used by a madman to destroy people on the ground. Its introduction is given as a violation of the sanctity of a natural cathedral on the ground. The opening paragraph of the book unfolds the sacredness of the surroundings:

One of Nature's oddities was the grove of six cabbage-trees in the dense shade of which Detective-Inspector Bonaparte had made his noonday camp. They grew beside an unmade road winding like a snake's track over a range of low, treeless and semi-barren hills; and, so close were they, and so virile their foliage, that to step in among them was not unlike stepping into an ivy-covered churchporch on a brilliant summer morning.

Bonaparte, safely inside the cool of this natural grove looks out at the events transpiring outside through a picture "framed within a leafy arch of Gothic type." While around him two crows, unaware of his existence but fearing him far less than the approaching terror caw and flutter; then as the plane drops a bomb inside the grove the crows "shrieked defiance" as the plane passed low above them, and the crows "left their sanctuary, and fleeing as though pursued by ten thousand hawks" they fled from their sanctuary. Bony, stunned though unhurt by the bombing reacts naturally and animal-like to the attack of the silvery-gray, unmarked plane in which one person sits. His "fine lips were drawn taut, revealing his white teeth in what was almost an animal snarl of fury." Thus, the lines are drawn for developing the story between the human-animal cunning of Bonaparte and the devil in the supernatural airplane. The result, though not one of Upfield's finest books, is a powerful statement of the supernatural aspects of man-made nature.

Upfield's second use of a supernatural symbol is of a different kind, less Christian but more heroically supernatural. And this book, living up very fully to the promise of the symbol, is perhaps his most powerful. *The Will of the Tribe* turns on Bony's greatest problem, whether as mediator between the two civilizations, white and aboriginal, he should give in to one or the other. In other words, the tug between the two which he and his author, Upfield, read as wrenching the country and the two cultures apart every day. This book is Upfield's most anguished examination of the struggle, and in this one, though not in others, Upfield and Bony come down on the side of the aborigines.

In a crater called Lucifer's Couch, created three hundred years ago by a falling meteor a dead white man is discovered by a plane load of people flying over. The crater had been fearfully avoided by natives for years. Now, however, the cosmically created cause of tension, or a symbol of tension, between the whites and the aborigines must be studied in order to catch the murderer. The supernatural symbol is subsumed under a more mundane but omnipresent symbol of civilization vs. naturalness, and is given social ramifications by virtue of the fact that a group of politicians have descended upon the environs to investigate the murder.

Throughout his series of books, Upfield, like Thomas Carlyle and many others before and after him, especially those prone to see symbols, uses a dominant symbol in depicting freedom vs. restraint, happiness vs. civilization, the aborigine vs. the civilized: clothes. Nakedness is natural, wearing clothes is civilized and unnatural. In one way or another, to one degree or another, in all the books where he is contrasting abos against whites, Upfield uses the figures of dressedness and undressedness. Aborigines wear as few clothes as possible, civilized whites wear many clothes. Where the abo must wear something to hide his nakedness, he should wear feathers, a natural kind of covering, but not the clothes of the whites. In the powerful study of the power of primitiveness and of tribal customs, *The Bone is Pointed* the witch doctor and others of the tribe, when they were casting their spell were "entirely naked save for the masses of feathers about his feet" (p. 139). In *The Mystery of Swordfish Reef* (1939), Upfield, who has admitted that on the sea Bony is outside his element, more vulnerable, is therefore more likely to present his symbols in their starkest strength. Such is his presentation of the clothes metaphor. Mr. Rockaway, a Jekyll-and-Hyde character whose obsession is, significantly, swordfishing, is trying to destroy Bony, who, however, has escaped and is sneaking upon Rockaway from the rear to destroy him for the pain and suffering he has inflicted upon others. Bony's garb is the ultimate in reversing to the natural state: "His general appearance was the antithesis of that of the being known to his colleagues. The veneer of civilization, so thin in the most gently nurtured of us, was entirely absent. He was wearing nothing. A film of oil caused his body to gleam like new bronze. His hair was matted with blood. His eyes were big, and the whites were now blood-shot. His lips were widely parted, revealing his teeth like the fangs of a young dog."

In *The Will of the Tribe* the role clothes play is even more extended and dramatic.

The kind and civilized Brentner family with two daughters of their own have taken into their family a beautiful abo girl, Tessa, ten years older than the daughters. The family plans for Tessa, who is treated like the white people, to go to college, which is unheard of for an abo, and then to become a school teacher. Tessa generally dresses in white, like the rest of the family. On the farm there is another aborigine, a young man, two years older than Tessa, who is called Captain, and is treated almost like a member of the family, surely with the same respect that other members of the working crew are accorded. He too dresses in white.

Nakedness and naturalness, or the lack of it, is the dominant theme in the plot. The countryside around the farm is described as "naked" therefore natural though barren. The aborigines are always being reprimanded for walking around naked, even without the customary feathers on their feet.

Tessa and the Captain represent two degrees of nativeness. She is trying to get away from it, the Captain, on the contrary, trying to conform to it and retain it. Yet in her reluctance to be entirely separated from her background, Tessa collects legends of the aborigines. The Captain is writing a history of his people. She is treating the subject nostalgically and romantically; he is treating it realistically. Bony, as the plot unfolds, is torn between the two points of view. He commends Tessa for her accomplishment: "You are a remarkable girl, Tessa" he told her, and she accepted the compliment with natural ease. Bony elaborates his point of view: "You know, there have been situations in my career when I've found myself acting as a kind of bridge spanning the gulf between the Aboriginal and the white mind. If you realise your ambitions you might well build a far stronger bridge, because you are thinking as a white woman." He explains his situation: "I am only half black, and yet I, too, have felt the pull towards my mother's race. It's tremendously powerful...." The Captain has already decided to serve his people; in fact he never toyed with the idea of serving any other.

Bony is torn between these two forces, his head telling him that one serves best by being outside the tradition, his heart telling him that instead one serves best by being within and a part of the system. The solution of the plot of the book and the resolution of this dilemma turns on clothes as a symbol.

Tessa, though the sweetest of individuals and trying hard to be white, cannot wear her two traditions without much personal conflict. She dresses immaculately, yet, like an aborigine woman, she is likely to swing her hips around men to attract their attention. She admits she is vain and enjoys being stared at. The Captain, loving Tessa, thinks that the clothes keep her too far from him, representing too much civilization for a young aboriginal woman; he resents them.

This particular tension of the book is released in one of the most dramatic and bizarre episodes in literature. The Captain, caught as being guilty of having killed the white man found in Lucifer's Couch, turns a gun on Bony and Tessa, telling her that she is his lubra (his woman). She, not sure she wants to give up civilized life, starts to run from Captain. He follows. Now the role of clothes becomes dominant. Tessa, realizing that she has become soft wearing white woman's clothes and shoes, realizes that if she is to escape from Captain she must discard her clothes. Captain, refusing to allow Tessa to get away, chases after her. During the chase, Tessa, in order to escape, first strips her skirt off, then, not being able to outrun the man, she stops and pulls her slip over her head. Then she pulls off her blouse and her bra. When she is virtually naked, feeling the cool air about her body, she feels free. "She knew she had regained what they said was her second wind, and another glance behind her showed her Captain was losing the race."

But she has not won the race for her life, and is not sure that she wants to. As she runs, she thinks over her past life and realizes that "the clothes she had worn for so long, the books and the study, the ambition to become a teacher, it hadn't been real after all. It was all a story told her by someone.... She was an Aborigine."

In her ears rings "her mother's voice, and the voices of all the women in the world.

"Now you know what to do if you are caught away from camp by a strange Aborigine, they said."

And Tessa, hearing this admonition, reaches down and pulls off her "beautiful green silk panties" and then collapses upon "the sandy ground and clawed the sand over her breasts and between her thighs."

In her mad chase to achieve what she thought was freedom, Tessa has turned several times toward Lucifer's Couch, feeling that in its confines she can hide and be protected—is calling on demonic assistance. But each time the supernatural assistance she is seeking is denied, and the natural life of the Aborigines pursues and eventually catches up with her. And she is glad. She becomes Captain's lover and his love. It is not a union of unequals, but of equals. The man and woman, now together, ran, not fast, "but together," toward what is obviously the accomplishment of the Aborigines, life in the traditional style. Bony knew that "Tessa had surrendered to the elfin call of her people, had put from her the slowly built influences of white assimilation, even as she had discarded the white-woman's clothes."

But Upfield wants to give Tessa another chance to relinquish the life of the aborigine. He is not sure Tessa has made up her mind, and not sure that he wants her to make that choice. So Bony brings her a new set of clothes which she puts on. He "calculated that now, as she dressed in clothes she had been educated to wear with distinction the primitive woman would be conquered by the sophisticated girl of the homestead." But with her mind now made up for the return to Aboriginal life, Tessa will not revert from her reversion, for her clothes are now ill-fitting and uncomfortable. These clothes "without the foundations, the smartly-cut skirt and the light-blue blouse made her pathetic," but her reversion is not complete. As they gather around a campfire to boil tea, Tessa at first squatted on her heels, as a lubra does, but then remembered, "correcting herself by sitting on the grounds and tucking her knees under the skirt."

But despite the momentary glance back into civilization, Tessa had made the decision she wanted. She tells Bony that she and Captain had had their way with each other: "We ran together into Eden by the back door." That does not mean that she has given up her civilized way of life, just properly proportioned it. After she and Captain are married, she remains at the homestead to help out, in a position hardly changed from that she had held before the great trauma, but not with the plans to become a school teacher and act as an intermediary between her race and the white one.

What does this episode in what is perhaps Upfield's strongest book really mean? This is the next to the last book that he finished, and his concluding statement on the subject, after a lifetime of observing and worrying. Was Upfield, after all, a sexist? Did he believe that a woman's place was on the reservation? This is his most obvious and powerful statement of such an attitude. Surely he is saying that civilization is not beneficial for the Aborigines. In *Man of Two Tribes* (1956) he says that "Eighty per cent of tribal strife has its origin in white interference" (p. 16). He is certainly interested in advancing the cause of the Aborigines, Bony's great ambition in life, and he may well believe that the cause can best be served by working from within. It would seem that he is denying Tessa the goal in life that she at least at one time thought she would enjoy and deserved. He is not saying that the two races can't mix; Bony was himself a half-breed and knew many others, who were exemplary and useful citizens. And he painted many full-blooded aboriginals as scoundrels. One thing is clear. Despite a life of wandering the Australian continent, or because of it, Upfield, like Bony, seemed to prefer order to chaos. Bony admired General Napoleon Bonaparte, for whom he was named, since Napoleon "never lost a battle because he planned against the future." Maybe Upfield felt it was easier to plan ahead in one's established role in society, to work from the inside out, evolutionarily rather than revolutionarily. As he had declared earlier, in *Bony and the Black Virgin* "Complete assimilation isn't achieved by the aborigine via swift passage from one State to another.... Assimilation is gradual and requires several generations" (p. 144)

But there can be no question that Upfield was not anti-feminist. Though he had some difficulty picturing real-life women, he was not alone. Most men have this difficulty regardless of their attitude toward liberated women. In one book in particular, *Madman's Bend* (1963), Upfield had pictured the evils of men and the strength of women. In this book, Lush is a drunken beast who abuses his wife and step-daughter. He is shot, and all evidence points to the step-daughter, who had the gun, the desire, and actually fired the gun through a door directly at her step-father. Although Upfield obviously hates Lush, he uses the book to point out the strength of women, especially young women. There can be no doubt where Upfield stands on the question of the strength of women.

Whatever philosophical and sociological conclusion one can draw from Upfield's books on this particular subject, and it surely must be positive, one must recognize that Upfield always wrote first-class heroic novels which turned on some kind of crime. He created one of the most remarkable detectives in crime fiction, a humanist who worked toward the betterment of society. In his half dozen superior books, Upfield created works of such power that they must be ranked with the finest and most respected works of not only crime fiction but of heroic literature of all kinds.

Peter Corris:
Sydney, Australia, Private Eye

Australia has not produced a writer of detective fiction who does for the urban areas what Arthur Upfield did for the vast out-back. In fact, such an author would be hard to find in any literature, Australian or otherwise, for Upfield, as we have seen, spoke for Australia, for all of the Continent except the urban coastal areas, and for all the vocations of the country, except those limited to the cities. But in the small library of Australian detective fiction there is one author who does treat the urban areas—specifically the tenderloin district of Sydney—comprehensively and well. That author is Peter Corris.

According to the scant information available in the United States about Corris, he is a former academic historian who decided that there is more money and pleasure in journalism and in writing detective and thriller fiction than in understanding and teaching the past. During the '80s so far, Corris has published some eight books and a collection of short stories. Obviously one of the major voices in contemporary Australian detective fictions, he resembles the older Arthur Upfield in at least one way. One of Corris' books, *The Winning Side* (1984), is about a part-Aborigine named Charlie Thomas who was born in a humpy camp in the 1920s and who through necessity learns early to fight in order to protect himself. After early years of boxing, Charlie joins the army, becomes a decorated veteran. When he returns to Australia he discovers that the prejudice that existed when he left has subsided only very little, so again he has two battles to engage in—the unadmitted one against his kind of people, and the admitted ones in the persons of his boxing opponents. Because of tenacity, good sense and good will, Charlie personally overcomes many of the battles of both rings.

Corris' study of the aborigine in a white society is hard-nosed and worthy. Without muffling his blows, he discusses Australian prejudice against Aborigines and half-castes. He talks about the very hard existence such people generally lead, and how difficult it is for them to escape it. The situation comes alive and is credible under Corris' pen. That should be enough for most readers. Unfortunately, for those who insist on thorough character development and what they might call verisimilitude, this book falls just a little short. The battles that the half-caste fights, the way he wins them, and the character of the man himself are somewhat out of kilter with reality. But often that happens with authors, and the case could be made that such negative criticism is obviated under the heavier accomplishment of this work.

Charlie Thomas is no Napoleon Bonaparte, and so far Peter Corris is no Arthur Upfield. But, again the comparison of the authors and characters is valuable only if the reader keeps in mind the vast difference in background and purpose between the two authors. In such a light Corris' study of the Aborigine as outcast in his own homeland makes a valuable contribution to a literature that in the past generally has avoided the subject.

Corris' urban mysteries are somewhat more successful as "literature." All center on the tenderloin section of Sydney, that is the areas near or related to Kings Cross, where the pubs, prostitutes, pimps and penniless hang out or where big money is made in underground activities. In all stories, the Private Investigator is a man named Cliff Hardy, a hard-nosed, fast-footed tough but by no means invulnerable witty person who works for pay but at times pays a great deal for the work he gets. In his stories there is, as the Sydney *Morning Herald* said about *Empty Beach* (1983), "the tang, often the sour tang, of inner Sydney, the hot and humid streets which may be corrupt but are never mean." It is a part of the city that Corris and apparently many Sydneyites love.

In at least one book, *Pokerface* (1985), Corris tries yet another genre, that of the spy thriller, with somewhat mixed success. A man is sacked from his job with the shadowy Federal Security Agency and his marriage is failing. He takes up with a punk group in order to try to clear his name because he thinks his former boss is manipulating him within the government.

The story line is good potential for a strong spy thriller. But thrillers depend more on action than on words; that is, words describe action but should not become substitutes for them. In *Pokerface* Corris, after the experience of writing mysteries, which depend more on words than actions, allows his talent for the mystery to overweigh that needed for the thriller, and this book therefore is not the success it might otherwise have been. Set in Melbourne, and connected with the government in Canberra, if tenuously, *Pokerface* is a good picture of one seamy side of Australian life. But it lacks the tensions that powerful thrillers possess. In the world of the detective mystery Corris has much more strength.

The term "meanness," of course like beauty, depends on the vocabulary of the beholder. The streets of Sydney that Hardy works are by no means safe. They are filled with hoodlums, drunks and murderers and the weapons these people use to eliminate their opposition range from knives to machine guns, dope and muscle. All of the books in the Cliff Hardy series are liberally sprinkled with these kinds of characters and activities. The streets are without doubt very dangerous.

Hardy, the private investigator, is no hero in the conventional sense we have been using in this book. On the contrary, he is only a survivor. Generally in every physical combat he comes away after having been kicked in the groin, bashed on the head, trussed up and cached away somewhere for an extended period of time. As a result of his jobs, Hardy is always a wounded and sore man.

To take an example, *The Empty Beach* (1983), one of Corris' early books, deals with a wealthy and successful man who has disappeared and whose wife wants him found, or at least wants to be sure that he is dead so that she can live her own life as surely and independently as she desires. Singer's activities before his disappearance are somewhat suspect, for they impinged upon the underworld in too many places and too frequently to be merely incidental. Though paid well for his work, with the promise of more fruitful dalliance always at the end of every paragraph, Hardy has enough of this adventure. At the end of the book, after it has been pretty definitely decided that Singer has in fact been killed, when Mrs. Singer says that she is not sure that her husband is not off in Bangkok, after plastic surgery, playing around with the native girls and that she will pay Hardy fifty thousand to investigate, Corris, with the rather wry humor that he frequently uses, has Hardy definitely turn down the assignment. He has been beaten up enough for one client.

This book also states the theme that constantly occurs in the Corris books: that the people Hardy works with are not one hundred percent normal, and that in dealing with them, Hardy reveals his lack of normality. Here Hardy quotes his ex-wife on his vocation: " 'You deal with damaged people,' she'd told me, 'because you're damaged yourself. You can't operate with normal, decent people.' " According to her, Hardy "mauled the decent people unless [he] was drunk, when he'd make fun of them to their faces." He therefore belonged in jail, along with the people he got sent there. Such is the interesting leitmotif heard in the bass section of all of these works.

Another example of his work, *Make Me Rich* (1985), is typical and is in many ways the most interesting of the books so far. In it Hardy is invited to come to the party of a rich beautiful lady to guard the valuables and to see that the drunks don't get overly aggressive. For the job he is to be paid $500. While overseeing the paintings, Hardy meets a woman named Helen Broadway, whom he finds interesting, and a man named Paul Guthrie who wants him to look for his step-son, Ray. Hardy's activities with Helen are necessarily constantly shelved while he looks for the step-son, who it turns out has taken up with a group of dope smugglers and outlaws. Hardy mixes with them, as he must in order to locate Ray. Generally quick with the repartee, quick to realize the value of flight when death is staring him down, Hardy notices all the life about him, understands it, works in it but is not necessarily a part of it. Sin, in fact, does not obsess his life; he constantly mentions incidentally that he has not had a woman in a long time.

His adventures are interesting and amusingly told. Corris' style is invigorating, somewhat similar to vintage American hard-boiled. For example, Corris describes a visit to a pub's toilet:

> A visit to the toilet depressed still further: the authenticity that was overwhelming—overwhelming old drains, authentic cracked bowls, authentic mould. The tiled floor was a Sargasso Sea of soggy cigarette-ends and discarded paper towels. A blood-encrusted sock was lying in a corner near the urinal and a trail of smeared, bloody footprints led to one of the cubicles.
>
> The mirrors in places like that are not for the vain. I washed my hands in the thin trickle of rusty water, and looked up at a man with crinkly dark hair, a broken nose and deep grooves in his cheeks. He bared his teeth at me and said, 'Cliff, you're starting to look as if you belong in a place like this.' I wanted to think of something smart to say to put him in his place but I couldn't. It was a relief to leave him there and go back up to the better company in the bar.(pp. 41-42)

As was said on a different situation by a different kind of person, Corris has the right words for the hard-boiled writer but is slightly off-key in his tune. But the writing is effective.

Deal Me Out (1986), begins on a matter of seeming less importance than those of the other books but ends up in a complex activity of great moment. Hardy is called in to investigate when the owner of

Bargain Renta Car, Terry Reeves, discovers that the cars he rents for a few days are never returned. The loss of the cars and the added cost of insurance are about to put him out of business. The plot gets mixed up with an author named Bill Mountain, who writes for TV and for the popular market—and owns but apparently does not read such international authors as Michael Lewin, Sjowall and Wahloo, and Maigret and turns around a scene in which Hardy is so well secured that Houdini could not have escaped, but he does. In this story Corris introduces a new kind of woman, for him, Erica Fong, and more sex than usual. He, of course, solves the problem of the missing cars and guarantees that the practice will not continue, at least with this gang of operatives.

This book is written with a lighter tone, perhaps a greater success of skill, than the earlier ones. There is a light spoof floating throughout, and it is amusing. That is not to say that the Private Eyeing is not as serious here as in the other books. It is. But it is as though Corris has decided to see if he cannot have a different kind of fun in this book. And he succeeds. The book fulfills both the desire of the reader interested in the activities of the Private Eye, and that of the persons who are interested in what some people in Australia read and take seriously.

Nevertheless, these two-thirds of a dozen books, published by Unwin Paperbacks, and perhaps a little difficult to get in this country, are well worth the reading. Although the setting is Sydney, the locale is anywhere in the world. The people are the same types, their activities universal, the problems facing humanity without limitations. Corris is an author who deserves a wide reading in the United States.

In 1985 Corris published *The Big Drop* and other short stories. In these the vintage Corris is very evident. The violence is more violent, the plots are more bizarre and thicker, and the action, as it would have to be in short stories, faster. The panorama of subjects for these stories is fascinating. In one, there is a smuggling gang in Sydney who simultaneously floods the market with bogus notes and with legitimate notes that have had the blue ink leeched from them. One story concerns counterfeit erotic sex pictures. Through all, there hovers a faked philosophy of Cliff Hardy, a toughness which he does not really feel and which he evidences nowhere except in these short stories, that he takes money from crooks, that is hot money, because he understands the world and how it operates: afterall, he says, he had no "qualms" about how money had been earned—"hell," he says, "I've worked for doctors and lawyers; all manner of professional people." Generally, however, in his novels Hardy makes an effort to distinguish more closely between the bad guys and the good guys and usually he succeeds.

The Heroic World
of Judson Philips

Judson Philips (1903-) is different in his writing in many ways from Arthur Upfield. Whereas Upfield is reserved, gentle and restrained in his style, Philips in his several voices is hard, violent, very supercharged in his attitude and statements. The two worlds the two authors write about are, of course, quite different. Rural Australia, even with crime in it, is more than half a world away from violent New York City and its environs.

Yet both authors have a great deal in common. Both are very much aware of their environments, and both write their books *in situo* and in reaction to their environments. Neither would make sense outside his locality. Yet each, in his own way, with his own style and own attitude, makes a great deal of sense in the world he is writing about. Each writes of a hero or of heroes that combat the evil they find around themselves.

Judson Philips who also writes under the names of Hugh Pentecost, Philip Owen, and others, has some 85 books to his credit and is still publishing novels and short stories. He is becoming one of the most prolific of American writers. His series characters are Luke Bradley, Pierre Chambrun, George Crowder, John Jericho, Lieutenant Pascal, Julian Quist, Grant Simon, Dr. John Smith, most of whom he has developed at times in both novels and short stories. Essentially all are used to examine Philips view of society; all tend to complement one another and round out what might be called a full profile of the unusual, heroic detective. All have some kind of "fatal flaw" or something unusual which sets them apart from society or makes them somewhat "different." Julian Quist is an "ace public relations man" and as such has to deal with all kinds of unusual people in show business. George Crowder, known locally as "Uncle George," has his life clouded by the fact that earlier on as Public Prosecutor he caused an innocent man to be condemned and executed. Peter Styles is the classic maimed defective, a physical cripple who turned detective in order to revenge himself on those persons who had maimed him; John

31

Jericho is a "Viking warrior" out of another age. Pierre Chambrun is the manager of the Beaumont Hotel, "New York's top luxury hotel," the home of the beautiful and rich people.

Of the phalanx of warriors serving law and order, Julian Quist in a dozen novels is perhaps the least distinctive and significant. As public relations man he must serve the best interests of his clients, but as citizen he also becomes embroiled in acts of crime perpetrated against society and his clients, often his clients being accused of the crimes. In *Party Killer* (1985) the agent is manager Larry Lewis, a diminutive, clownish comedian who has the perverse notion of inviting all four of his former wives to a celebration at his place. One by one they are murdered, and accusations naturally fall his way. He seems to be the only one with a motive for getting rid of them, though the motive is not apparent. In a somewhat fumbling (that is natural) manner Quist aids in discovering the murderer. Because these are relatively unheroic accomplishments by rather natural people, this series is perhaps Philips' most natural kind of writing. The people are rather believable, the actions almost natural, and Philips' style of writing most moderate, that is without the fire and brimstone of some of his other series, and therefore to some readers quite enjoyable.

In the "Uncle George" series of five novels, Philips becomes more heroic. George Crowder as country attorney had flawed his life by convicting a man of homicide when he was in fact innocent, and having him executed. Though no one blamed George for presenting his case as effectively as possible, the event shattered his life. He disappeared, and years later appeared again in his former hometown, this time a man with a great mysterious background and a heavy burden on his shoulders, his life "completely turned around," despite the fact that he is a hero to all the people in his home town and is called "Uncle George."

In *Murder Sweet and Sour* (1985) George's beloved sister, Esther, has been kidnapped from a shopping center parking lot, and her husband, Hector, and their son, Joey, come to "Uncle George" for help in locating her. Through a series of blind alleys and skillfully devised clues, George and Hector search the countryside. In the end it is Hector and Joey who rescue her. George is quite happy to give credit for the rescue to Hector, whom in the past he has despised but now has developed a great respect for, and Joey, who has always hero-worshipped his uncle. He is delighted to see them rise in their own eyes and in those of the community.

The series about George as hero are, like those books about Quist, less heroic and flamboyant than the series about some of Philips' other heroes. Mild tempered, mild styled, they pretty much picture language and life as it is, at least in fiction. As such they, again, are quite interesting, perhaps more interesting than the Quist books, though Philips seems to have a fatal attraction for the beautiful people.

The Protective Violence of Peter Styles

Throughout history the physically deformed, mentally or emotionally unusual person—the maimed, deformed, freakish, giant, dwarf, extraordinarily beautiful and talented, grotesquely ugly and evil, the mentally disturbed—have been considered to have been smiled or frowned on by the gods and therefore to possess some special dispensation or power. Mythology and folklore are rife with this tradition. "Monsters" were reported by the astrologers of Nineveh and Babylon three thousand years ago. In detective fiction the hero, the protagonist, has always been a bit unusual. Auguste Dupin and Sherlock Holmes as heroes continued the tradition. During the 1930s and '40s in America the pulp detective heroes were very unusual; one had no face, one would lose his sight just when it was needed most, one was an amnesiac, one had to crawl on the floor because of his deformed body, and there were scores of others; but they always got their criminals.

Today the tradition of the maimed detective continues to run strong. Perhaps the reasons are clear. Our social, political and economic conditions are similar to those of the Great Depression and today these detectives serve the purposes of those of the earlier period. Or perhaps one might speculate that when society is threatened, as it always is in crime fiction, the veneer of compassion slips easily off the law of the people and the predator takes advantage of the weak. Further, in time of social and economic conflict the elite, artificial trappings of the so-called civilization rub off and people revert to the apparently everlasting truth of mythology and folklore as our reactions to the conflicts of life. When we do, we call upon the types of oldest tradition—the maimed hero—to aid and protect us. The "freak" tradition is manifest in various writers today. Sometimes it is subordinated or seems only incidental, as in G.W. Grafton's *The Rat Began to Gnaw the Rope* (1983), where the detective says on one occasion: "Every person has some cross to bear. Mine is that I am not shaped like other people who are intended to get their clothes in ready-to-wear shops." In Steve Allen's latest book, *The Talk Show*

Murders (1982) the detective has a nose larger than Jimmy Durante's (and Sherlock Holmes') and his black female chief assistant sings "sideways." There is a blind detective (Duncan McLain), one who is deaf (Samson Trehune), one who has selective amnesia (Nick Caine) and one who utilizes the extrasensitivity that comes from his being an identical twin, one of whom is evil (William D. Blankenship's *Brotherly Love*, 1981). Michael Collins' (Dennis Lynds') Dan Fortune, a hard-boiled detective with only one arm has survived in ten books now. The latest, *Freaks* (1983) has Fortune constantly beaten up by his adversaries and loved by women for his unusualness. Another "freak" today is George C. Chesbro's Mongo, a 4 ft. 6 in. dwarf, who is a renaissance man, a Ph.D. professor at a New York City university, former circus performer and black-belt expert, and a detective.

Philips' Peter Styles is a physical "cripple" who turned detective in order to revenge himself on those persons who maimed him. A reluctant participant in the world of crime who came from a brilliant career as a magazine writer, Styles is more the vigilante than the detective. But in seeking his personal revenge he has to do a lot of detecting, which benefits other victims of hate and violence. His is not the sexual violence of Mike Hammer, who was operating at the same time, but a personal-social violence. He is directly in line with but is a more sophisticated version of the vigilante detective of pulp fiction of the 1930s and '40s. He acts out the concept of purification through powerful action so much a part of the American fiber of life, as charted by Richard Slotkin in his book *Regeneration Through Violence*.

Like the birth of all classic detectives, Styles was, like Shakespeare's Caesar, torn from his parent's womb, in this case his father's; and like Oedipus he had to slay his father before he could become his own tormented self.

Before his second birth of freedom from his father, Styles had served a painful tour in Korea. While there he became increasingly alarmed at the antics of his father, Herbert, who when his wife, Styles' mother, died gave up his successful career and began drinking himself into oblivion. Styles, when he returned to America determined to reform his alcoholic father but was unable to do so. Finally, in desperation, one weekend Peter determined to drive his father to a health resort and talk him into reforming.

On the mountain road leading to the resort, Styles and his father were overtaken by a supernatural agent in the form of two young men who had "demonic" laughter and were "thrill killers" determined to destroy anyone they could. Styles fought them for the road, growing ever more annoyed and intemperate over their behavior. He was determined that they not force him to bend to their demonic will. Increasingly, as they sped down the road the battle for the control of the will became supernaturalized.

Peter Styles is in a "cold fury." He argues with his father who is "shaking like a man with palsy." Peter won't listen to his father's pleading to "let them by." Since his son won't listen to him. Herbert tries to reassert his manhood and parenthood by grabbing the wheel, and in so doing, apparently realizing his failure to become again the man and father, seemingly deliberately destroys them both: "Herbert reached out and grabbed the wheel. Instead of pulling them to the inside of the road he somehow managed to turn the wheel to the left." He drives them off the road, down a long embankment and in a funeral pyre the flaming car incinerates the father but breaks Peter's leg, causing the right leg to have to be amputated below the knee (*The Laughter Trap*, 1964, p. 18). This physical maiming twists Styles' personality. The experience became a "nightmare" and though the accident had actually "freed" him from the problems of his father, revenge became an obsession. The mythic nature of the revenge quest, worldwide in literature, echoes the calamity of the Wandering Jew of worldwide folklore who can never find a cessation of his wandering and searching for death. Styles struggles "with the cold rage that sent him hunting for the two laughing men who were responsible, a hunt that ended forever in failure." Styles always felt that "someday, in his war against meaningless violence, he would lose. He had always imagined it as an heroic moment" (*Thursday's Folly*, 1967, pp. 78, 165).

Styles wants to extirpate all violence in the world and replace it with universal compassion and love, love of men and women for all other people, and for personal love. The books about this quest are most peculiar anomalies. They begin in violence and race through it in a degree of action perhaps equaled today only by such writers as Robert Ludlum and Frederick Forsyth, whose main purposes in their books are action and violence. Philips' Peter Styles novels are like tensely coiled steel springs tightened almost to the breaking point, about to snap and destroy everything around them. Philips (who lives in New Canaan, Connecticut) has always been interested in the theatre; and his books are theatrical.

Styles' strength and hate of his maimed conditions emphasize his superhuman qualities. He has a nearly perfect mechanical ankle and foot, and walks with hardly a noticeable indication of his physical condition. Yet Philips uses this mechanical gadget to emphasize Styles' humanism by showing how much he hates the mechanism. It diminished his manhood, his own personal manhood and thus makes him less capable of love and understanding. Styles tries to avoid talking about the part; he will let no one see it. When someone else handles the contraption, Styles feels physically violated, his manhood having been attacked and diminished. Once (*The Laughing Trap,* pp. 88-9) he is drugged and put to bed by an unknown person while he is knocked out. The thought that his stump was seem by unfriendly eyes tore him apart: "The thought that he had been ¢handled' had brought back feelings of shame about his leg that he'd thought he'd lived down a long time ago. He wondered what thoughts his nocturnal visitor had had when he saw the stump of the leg with its flushed, pink flesh. What comments? Had they laughed at him? They could have felt nothing but contempt for him in his helplessness.

Sooner or later someone was going to pay for that period of pleasure. It was a moment which he would never forgive or forget."

The importance of the amputated part to Styles' personality and to all the people around is symbolically emphasized in its sexual overtones. Styles is constantly asked by other men if women don't find it a special asset. Once (*Hot Summer Killings,* 1968, p. 88) a black man asks: "How do women go for that stump?... I bet they love it. They always go for something a little off beat. I bet you've got all kinds of tricks you can do with it." But Styles himself feels quite the reverse: "He had never been able to convince himself that any woman could live with the mutilation without feeling pity or unwilling revulsion." In fact, however, he need not have worried. The black man is right. Women love the thought of sex with this man. For example, in *The Laughter Trap,* the leading lady, although she is married to Peter's best friend, tell Styles about her and other women's availability: "All you have to do is say that you want me or any other woman."

Generally Philips' books are not conventional detective books. Instead they are about terrorists who try in one way or another to control people by coercion or extortion. Styles undertakes a superhuman quest to right these wrongs. His is a lonely and dangerous task. Often the wrongs are sanctioned by the society, or sections of it, that he is dedicated to protect.

In *Whisper Town* (1960), for example, the right wing elements of a small town—in collusion with a fascistic sheriff—is trying to destroy a schoolteacher for teaching sex education in high school. Styles exposes the threat. In *Hot Summer Killings* (1968), one of three books concerned with black-white relations, New York City is "sick with hate," and is about to be torched by rebellious blacks who have been manipulated one time too many by whites. A politician has siphoned off large amounts of money intended for improvement of poor blacks. At great risk to himself, Styles brings the blacks and whites together because he believes in justice and love. Styles asks if tension will cool off once the guilty white has been exposed: "It could.... But just for now, Styles. You people don't come alive to what we people got to have, and it will be just for now." The apocalypse lies certainly ahead.

In that strange anomalous thinking of his, Styles is against all lawlessness except his own excursions outside the law needed to restore law and order. He asks the Black if he has not learned that anarchy doesn't work for anyone. Apparently the black man has not; nor in fact has Styles.

Philips' books parallel others on the same subject written at the same time. For example, Ed Lacy's *In Black and Whitey* (1967) has New York City about to be torn apart by racial injustice and hatred, and Michael J. Kingsley's *Black Man, White Man, Dead Man,* (1969) has a small town in Kentucky split between blacks demanding their rights and repressive red-neck whites, including a corrupt police sergeant, determined to suppress these rights. Both books smolder with tense and explosive hatred but they are not so taut and consuming as Philips'.

In *Black City* (1964, pp. 77-78), Styles talks about the way to cure the diseases of the public and of individuals: "In 1963 the President was assassinated. I don't blame the psychotic unfortunate who pulled the trigger nearly as much as I blame the community where by reckless slander, bigotry and meaningless hatred a climate was created in which Lee Harvey Oswald thrived. The problem in my book is what to do about society at large, and not what to do about the results of their attitudes. Cure the disease, not the symptoms."

Styles' major cure for both symptoms and disease is love, both personal and societal. He personally is always seeking a love but believing he cannot find it. Finally he encounters personal love in the widow of his best friend—again raising the significance of his work into the superhuman by reestablishing a motif common in mythology and folklore: love in close-knit units and friends marrying and taking care of widows and widowers of deceased friends. In another book (*Nightmare at Dawn*, 1970), the universal need for love and compassion is emphasized. A little black boy who has witnessed a gang murder of a black man knows that he endangers his own life by reporting the murder, yet he does., Styles says: "If it had only been my safety, I wouldn't have allowed you to take the chance. But you see, there are so many others." One of Styles' friends answers" "I wish more of us could think in those terms." In another book (*Black Glass City*, 1964) after the city has been saved from the torch of hatred by blacks, a friend tells Styles, the magazine writer, "When you write your piece, ram it down their throats that we can't make our private worlds to live in. We have to live in the same world with everyone else, and by the same laws as everyone else. We can't make our own rules or invent our own moralities." Styles seems to agree, and this attitude is surely a major part of his thinking.

Philips' philosophy as verbalized and acted out by Peter Styles seems a strange contradiction and paradox. He is absolutely dead set against bigotry, right-wing attitudes and actions, private vengeance— anything that is against group compassion and love, the group and the individual. He is violently opposed to violence. He seems always to be acting alone, not so much *with* as *for* the public good. He seems like one of Ayn Rand's heroes who know perfectly well what the public needs. In setting society right, he is surely not inclined to turn the other cheek. If he did it would be stiffened with a frown and the turning would be followed by some kind of violence. Of all the evils in the world, perhaps none is more repugnant to Philips than the cannibalism with which strong people devour the weak— body and soul. The metaphor is much stronger than Frank Norris' figure of snakes in a glass enclosure devouring mice, because Norris' act is natural. Philips sees man eating man, woman and child as unnatural, and he reacts against it strongly. In *The Cannibal Who Overate* (1962), a book written under the name of Pentecost not including Peter Styles, Philips has an egomaniac writer who manipulates and destroys people in every way until he brings about his self destruction.

The battle in Philips' books is between giant cannibals of all sorts and the private individuals and the public's champion. In these convulsions of the battles of giants, Styles joins the heroes of old, like Beowulf, King Arthur, David, Robin Hood, Paul Bunyan, Davy Crockett and countless others. All of the combatants have their individualized weapons. Styles' too is unusual. It is not Beowulf's great strength, Arthur's Excalabar, Robin Hood's bow and arrow, Bunyan's great strength, Crockett's eye gouging, not David's sling. It is the detached ankle and foot of a writer and the righteous indignation that was caused by and goes with it. Seldom have parts of the body had more effect in fighting corruption and evil. With Styles one fights fire with fire, corruption with cleverness, violence with violence. An ankle and foot can be very violent—attached or unattached. It can be far more effective than Samson's jawbone of an ass!

The Fiery Viking, John Jericho

Of all his characters, Philips' John Jericho, written under the name of Hugh Pentecost, is the most obviously heroic. Detective fiction about private investigators is filled with men of huge size, most of them no taller than 6 feet four inches. Some, however, are somewhat larger. W.T. Ballard's Bert McCall is 6 feet 5 1/2 inches, S.S. Jaffrey's Colonial PI Captain Cord stands 6 feet 6 inches. In addition to this great size few PIs have red hair; Anthony Boucher's Fergus O'Breen has flaming red hair and green eyes. Pentecost's John Jericho, joining two traditions of the unusual, stands 6 feet 6 inches tall *and* has red hair and red beard. Jericho, carrying the Biblically resonant name from the Old Testament, stands tall as heroes did in the old sagas.

Pentecost emphasizes Jericho's heroic proportions. As he describes him:"It would be impossible for me to cast John Jericho in the current popular mold of the un-hero. His size and appearance would be against it from the start. He stands six feet six inches tall and weighs a good two hundred and forty pounds, without an ounce of extra fat. Add to that his thick red hair and his red beard and you don't have a man you pass by on the street without a second look. He is a Viking warrior out of another age" (*Hide Her From Every Eye*, 1966, p. 1). Jericho, like Styles, came of age as a fighter against injustice while serving in Korea. Jericho is a painter who "paints what he sees and feels in vivid colors. As a human being he is a sucker for the helpless, for the lost causes of individuals and groups." Jericho lives and paints like an angry man who always feels passionately. His are a combination of physical and emotional attributes that characterize the nearly-perfect modern hero. In developing this personality, Pentecost uses plots, organization and language somewhat different from those of the Peter

Styles series. Here the world is big, violent and starkly heroic; the language throbs with this attitude. Generally the verbs stand without modifiers, each a flexed muscle tensed to deliver an heroic message. The plots of the novels are distinctly individualized, allowing a sensitive artist adventures that allow his powers full play.

In the second novel of the series—*Hide Her From Every Eye*—the trouble in a small Connecticut town is that a young wife is caught up in a conspiracy of black-mail by a local man who cloaks his deeds under the pretense of only wanting to do good. The innocent wife is driven to alcoholism, and all the town's important people, including her husband, conspire to blame all the town's troubles on this wife, Marcia Potter in order to keep her drinking. The conspiracy of this group of people for their own selfish ends is a theme that consumes Pentecost throughout this series. In his book the intensity of the plot is given comic relief—and intensification—by one of Pentecost's finer minor creations—an elderly editor of the local newspaper who has written the local news for years to please the town while knowing what has usually gone on. Now he is fed up and yearning for justice in an unjust world and wants to write only the truth.

Like all heroes, Jericho has a weakness—or a strength, depending on your point of view—which is "his inclination to make facts fit a theory in which he currently believes" (p. 183). But, of course, this "weakness" always allows him to come forth at the end with the truth, as he does in this book.

If Pentecost himself has a weakness in developing the books about John Jericho it is trouble with the endings. With the heroes of tradition, the heroes settle the problems of the world because it is their role in life, and do not get emotionally involved. When they do get involved it is because they are human beings and must participate in the role of life to a certain extent. Jericho, however, is a giant with a giant's emotions and degrees of involvement. When society is cut, he bleeds, and he roars like a bleeding bull. All this has a life-like ring to it. But Pentecost apparently does not know how to let Jericho be such a participant in life and still not get himself tied down by its strings. In most books Jericho or Pentecost fails to see beyond the conclusion, and Jericho commits himself not to the next adventure but to the woman he has just saved. In *Hide Her From Every Eye*, for example, there is no cliff-hanger that will interest the reader in buying the next adventure of this modern hero (an understandable and justifiable device). Rather the hero tumbles off the cliff and commits himself and his future to the future of the woman he has rescued from unjust destruction. But Pentecost does not follow up with a sequel developing this relationship.

Another book of the same year— *The Creeping Hours,* 1966— lunges off into a new field for John Jericho but a continuing major concern for Pentecost—the problem of youth, this time youth caught up in the power of the television and movie empires. As the power of money conspires to chew up and destroy its performers, Jericho is called in to protect the participants. He is at his best. He fights the mob which throws in naked power when needed, he resists the power of sex—somewhat unusual for a man of his reputation—and remains true to his lot of calling a spade a spade.

In *Dead Woman of the Year* (1967), the fourth novel in the series, Jericho is called into the chic world of high fashion and lots of money— and the great violence that comes with trying to achieve and maintain the highest and richest of positions in that world. Lydia Trask was to be named "Woman of the Year" by *Tomorrow's World Magazine* but her competitors and enemies were brought in to start throwing acid into the faces of women who looked like her. Naturally, the horror of the situation brings in Jericho, and it is no major jump to the conclusion that Lydia Trask had been earlier associated with Jericho. In fact they had been married. This long arm of coincidence, however, does not nullify or vitiate the true suspense and power of the book. The strength of the city and money are compellingly portrayed and Jericho lives up to his reputation of being always brutally candid, generally unselfish, and always dedicated to the higher good of morality, society and humanity's well being. Unfortunately the ending is one of those conclusions which if taken seriously would prevent any more Jericho novels. Luckily, however, we readers have forgotten the ending when we take up the next John Jericho novel.

The next—*The Girl With Six Fingers* (1969)—turns on one of Pentecost's major interests, and one that he also develops in one of the Peter Styles novels—the conspiracy by the puritanical elders and sadistic fascists of a small Connecticut town against the youth of a different persuasion and attitude toward life. This time it is a Happening at which a girl is to appear naked and be painted in various and bizarre colors as a part of "instant esthetics." Naturally the Establishment is against such affronts to law and order and decency. Law and order in this case is personified in the obese figure of a benefactor who contributes to the churches, library and other statements of civic virtue so that he can control them. It is a case of great power used for selfish and sick purposes. Again, Jericho,

who must surely represent Pentecost's own attitude, fairly seethes at
the bigotry and presumptuousness that allow an individual to usurp
the church, society and even the police of a community. It is a subject
that Peter Styles railed against also.

In all, the Jericho series is remarkable. To a certain extent the
stories must stick to formula and develop along similar lines; for
example, the narrator uses exactly the same sentence in every novel
to describe and characterize John Jericho and his relationship to the
narrator. And of course Jericho acts in the same prescribed manner
that being the heroic Jericho he must act in. Nevertheless each book
is markedly different from all the others and decidedly interesting.
It is a worthwhile series about a remarkable hero written by an
individual who was literally at the strongest of his verbal, though
not esthetic, powers.

Pierre Chambrun—Ordinary Hero

In many ways the least unusual—and therefore the most
"realistic"—of the heroes is Pierre Chambrun, written under the name
of Hugh Pentecost. Protagonist in the novels, Chambrun is the
manager of the Beaumont Hotel, "New York's top luxury hotel."
He has as his assistant Mark Haskell, in charge of public relations
at the hotel.

In developing the goings on of the beautiful and powerful people
who frequent the Beaumont, Pentecost delves into the society and
personalities of this branch of elite society which throughout his works
is a major concern. In these examinations, however, Pentecost does
not bring the people into direct confrontation with the remainder
of society to the degree he does in other books.

The detective-hero, Chambrun, is in some ways the least unusual
of Philips' heroes, and in some ways is unlike all others. His
background varies somewhat from the ordinary—he was in the French
Resistance during World War II. Physically his size is undistinguished.
He is, as one of his former fellow Resistance fighters calls him, "a
little bastard" who "was the toughest of the lot" of the Resistance
fighters. In a later book (*Random Killer,* 1979), Pentecost fills out
the portrait. Chambrum is "a short, dark square little man with bright
black eyes burned in deep pouches, who can look like a compassionate
father-confessor or a hanging judge depending on his mood at the
moment. The Beaumont is *his* hotel," his city and his life.

This background hardly explains all of Chambrun's personal and business characteristics. Obviously insecure under the responsibility of the hotel on his shoulders, he compensates by a punctiliousness which makes him a slave of time and habit. He always has breakfast served to him in his office at 9 A.M. For him to vary is "no more unusual than to wake up at nine o'clock some day to find, on looking out the window that the sun had chose not to rise. (*Death After Breakfast*, p. 1). He always has his public relations man, Mark Haskell, appear in his office door at 9:45 A.M. on the dot. Chambrun always dines in his suite at 9 P.M. In addition, Chambrun always knows exactly what guests are in the hotel, what they are doing, and caters to their every whim until they begin to cast shadows on the spotless reputation of the hotel, at which time they must go. His care borders on invasions of privacy. He has cards on the public and private lives of guests which tell him instantly whether the guest can afford the hotel, whether he or she is a lush, what their sexual habits and preferences are, and such things. His own sexual habits are underlined in each book. Nobody knows whether he has any sex life because there is no evidence that he can take time from his job or has the inclination. In *The Deadly Joke* (1971), Haskell says that Chambrun is "married to the hotel." "But a man that's all man, like Pierre, must have a woman," says a lady Resistance fighter from the old days. "If he does, it is a very private matter," answers Haskell.

Perhaps the most revealing characterization of Chambrun is in his relation to one of his assistants, Miss Ruysdale, who though beautiful is always neat, trim, severely dressed and coiffured and "unruffled." Haskell, who tells all these stores, makes the point that although there is no evidence on the point, it is assumed by the hotel staff that there is some kind of sex life between Chambrun and Miss Ruysdale, but Haskell emphasizes the fact that Chambrun, for whatever reasons he might have, always "neuters" Miss Ruysdale by calling her simply "Ruysdale." This ambiguous sexual proclivity is particularly peculiar since Judson Philips, in his other books, obviously has nothing but contempt for any kind of man who is not one hundred percent male.

Chambrun is a friendly, warm person whom all his employees, and nearly all the people who use the hotel, like, admire and respect. Though a computer-mind programmed with all kinds of information which could compromise many of the people he knows, he is discreet, interested in maintaining the reputation of the Beaumont, advancing the lives and careers of his guests, and being an exemplary citizen.

In these struggles he dramatizes all the concerns of the author and perhaps more important the author's major concern with the role of the people who frequent the hotel, their impact on society and society's relation to them. Here, as in all of Pentecost's books, there is violence, or the threat of violence, though in these books there is frequently the hint or threat of it rather than the actuality.

In *The Cannibal Who Overate* (1962), the book that introduces Chambrun, Pentecost has not fully distinguished the manager of the Beaumont from his other detectives, especially John Jericho. This particular study turns on a maniacally egotistic author who will do anything to blow up his own reputation, keep himself in the public eye, hide the fact that his only literary success was in fact written by another person though published as his own work, and allow himself to coldly destroy all the people with whom he comes in contact; he is a monster who is a danger to all society, and Chambrun, though having much difficulty tracking down the intricate plot, arrives on the final scene just in time to prevent the mad author, named Aubrey Moon, from destroying his real intended victim and perhaps getting away scot free. Pentecost's denouement in this book—and in the series— lacks the indignant fire of his other series. As one of the characters comments, "It seems that at last our cannibal [the author who would "do anything to maintain his literary immortality"] has overeaten. Fill up the glasses.... I'd like to drink to that."

As Pentecost developed this series with characteristics markedly all his own, his general feeling about the classes of people represented and their responsibilities to one another is strengthened. In *The Evil That Men Do* (1966) this control is complete. In this book a rich and beautiful movie star member of the jet set checks into the Beaumont under one of her aliases—Dorothy Smith—though she brings with her the gang of socially and morally irresponsible fellow jet-setters known after her real name—Doris Standing— as "Standing's army." Pentecost's attitude can perhaps best be represented in a series of quotes.

"The stuffed shirt, as a member of society, is a pain in the neck," Chambrun said. "I think most of us rather enjoy the spectacle of a really Grade-A stuffed shirt taking a good pratfall in public. Doris Standing and her army make a crusade of staging public pratfalls for the overstuffed." But "Doris' army are like cats after tuna fish. They must have it...they must have their sardonic laughter [here shades of the sardonic laughter which echoed to the maiming of Peter Styles].... These people dig up unpleasant truths and expose them. They aren't blackmailers. They are so rich that money is meaningless.

They do what they do simply for the pleasure of inflicting pain" (pp. 20-21).

In developing here the same concern that he uses to power his prose about his maimed hero Peter Styles, Pentecost emphasizes the wanton viciousness of these worthless members of society. "They play games like children...vicious games. They laugh at honest sentiment. But it goes a lot deeper than this. They destroy genuine human relationships."

In traveling all over the world for their cruel purposes, these people recruit people of gigantic proportions who make the fight between them and the heroes of society all the more momentous. In this book, for example, three of the soldiers fighting for evil are an Englishman, a veteran of the Royal Air Force who "wasn't receptive to the rigid disciplines" of civilian life; another, a "giant of a man, physically, with a shock of carrot-colored hair...son of a wild Irish poet and a Dutch mother.... His record was a one way street of brawling and debauchery and simple-minded violence [a description narrowly close to that of John Jericho]; the third looked like Death itself: physically ugly, "He was short, with a hint of deformity in stooped, round shoulder. His hair was black, worn long so that it went down over the back of his collar in an unkempt fringe... His nose was large and beaked. His lips were thick and sagged to one side as if he might have had a stroke at some time (pp. 83-84).

Pentecost's control over his subjects continued to grow. By the time of *Death After Breakfast* (1978) the formula had rigidified and the tradition carried on with or without Chambrun. For the first half of this book, Chambrun is missing, having been kidnapped and taken to New Jersey. The hotel staff carry on in his absence because "his instructions were law," as Haskell says. The plot turns on the necessity of some Nazi film makers maintaining their secrecy in order to escape Israeli Nazi-hunters. Again, Pentecost is concerned with anti-social behavior and its being flouted, even by people who put political ideology and cause above all other motivations.

By the end of the 1970s, Pentecost had altered his formula a little, had expanded his geography and incorporated into the Chambrun story another of his obsessions. In *Random Killer* (1979) Pentecost continues the break with using Chambrun as the only investigator brains that he had started in *By Death After Breakfast*. In this later book it is important that some investigation be carried out in Colorado and Mark Haskell is sent to do it, though he will only be carrying out Chambrun's plan and organization.

Haskell does not finish the overall investigation, of course, since Chambrun must solve the murders back in his little hotel-world. But in shifting the geography to Colorado, Pentecost moves to that part of the country that was to predominate in the Peter Styles series. Further, the plot turns on the same kind of physical mutilation that created and motivated Styles. The murderer in *Random Killer* had been "shot down by Israeli commandos in an Arab town. The loss of his right leg crippled Conklin [the murderer] in more ways than one, psychologically as well as physically. Always successful with women, Conklin now felt mutilated, ugly, ashamed. He saw himself forever shut off from romantic seductions. He turned to the business of buying his sex from women who didn't care whether he had one leg or three, as long as he paid the price." Being maimed and alienated from society causes all kinds of desperate actions. It is perhaps significant that Pentecost develops the motivation of this enemy of society in precisely the same way that he does that of Peter Styles, who after his baptism in the fire of mutilation turns out to be a champion, not an enemy, of people. But because Conklin is evil, mutilation has an evil and alienating effect. Springing from similar social and physical backgrounds, people take different routes and developments in life, with startlingly different consequences.

The development of this Chambrun hero is perhaps based on a shaky premise since it revolves around a society that seemed without compassion and about a hero who might have been indifferent to others outside his microcosm of a world. But Chambrun is a successful character development. His development constitutes a kind of third of a total heroic concept, here more social than physical, that would be joined to the other two—Peter Styles and John Jericho— to help round out Judson Philips' picture of the role of the hero-detective in society. That they all sprang from the same mind is rather obvious in the parallel—though at times not close—development. Nevertheless, they are all distinct characters in distinct stories which spring from a reaction to society and which voice the feelings and needs of people in that society. As such they are effective social documents.

Ed Lacy:
Passage Through Darkness

Ed Lacy (Leonard S. Zinberg, 1911-1968), who as Steve April also wrote 28 novels and 100 short stories and as Len Zinberg another 6 novels, was a writer of many styles and purposes. In his books at times he is a run-of-the plot writer with a talent for fast, racy, hard-knuckle plots and for language that reads easily and is worth spending a small amount of money or time to obtain and an hour or two in the reading. These plots are generally conventional: his male leads are down-and-out hotel dicks and/or ex-police men, the women are generally hookers, professional or otherwise, or are ready to jump into bed with men though they are diseased, sick, ready to die, paranoid or otherwise undesirable. The plots are filled with violence, sometimes sado-masochistic, with very little of the humanity in them that makes people warm to other persons, that makes people cotton to a writer because of the message he is trying to put forth.

So on the surface Lacy bears little resemblance to Arthur Upfield. Upfield has his detective Bony say dozens of times that he is not interested in crime and violence; he is, on the contrary, interested in solving a crime because it offends his sense of pride that anyone can get away with not being caught. Once they are caught, however, Upfield's Bony is not really interested in seeing his law-breakers punished. He has studied the crime in a particular setting in Australia, has worked out the relationship between the geography and topography and the crime, and is generally content to let nature and man take their course. Lacy bears a much closer resemblance to Philips, however. Both write about the same part of the United States in general. Both have the same kind of characters in mind: their worlds are without doubt violent, their characters push violence to its very edge. Lacy and Philips differ in one important way, however. There is little ambivalence in Philips in his feeling toward the world and characters he writes about. In Lacy's fiction, however, there is even less equivocation.

Lacy's attitude toward his lead characters in his early books seems to be ambivalent, but it is non-heroic. As heroes, the main characters make fun of themselves, think they are what they really are (bums) and at times even act deliberately like people out to destroy any heroic image they might have created.

The style, however, is fast moving and effective. Take for instance a passage about the mandatory attitude of the men toward women and violence:

It was a nice bedroom, with pink drapes and candy-striped wallpaper. The bed had been slept in, the sheets were mussed, a dressing table and a couple of chairs were overturned and the dressing mirror smashed. The corpse lay on the bed, clothed in a blue silk negligee, a good deal of her naked, dead body showing—It had been a fairly interesting body, firm thighs. She was lying on her back and from what I could see, she'd been average pretty, maybe cute, for a dame in her late thirties. The back of her head was smashed in, her thick blonde hair messy with matted blood. A little metal table lamp lying near the head had evidently been the skullcracker *Sin in Their Blood*, (pp. 25-25).

The violence is induced by the times and the society. This is just after the Korean war and that is what caused people to turn to violence. In *Sin in Their Blood*, Matt, the hero, had been trained in Korea with a machine gun and to seeing all kinds of people, especially the aged and children, blown to pieces. This violence had created violence at home:

...America is becoming tough-punchy. In the movies a guy can't romance a gal without slapping her around; in the so-called comic books, violence is a big laugh. Even kids—little ones—go around packing toy guns. Toughness has become a...a...virtue, like honesty. When are are we going back to normal? Think of peace and love between people, stop trying so hard to be a nation of Humphrey Bogarts!" (p. 54).

The early characters, the heroes, take themselves very seriously— they are obsessed with their problems, their little worlds, and the dirty characters who inhabit them. It is difficult to see that Lacy takes them seriously. Yet he does. In their own little worlds these characters show some degree of compassion and empathy for their fellow human beings, but mainly because all are in the same gutter and need some love and compassion, or some sex and compassion. In *The Men from the Boys* Marty Bond is an ex-dick, down on his luck, forced to live as a hotel detective and to protect whores and to extort money from residences of the hotel under the least pretext. He actually cares for his women, however. And he is gargantuan He is stronger and more violent, and his obsessions with his own problems are larger than life. He lunges through life and against the evil characters of the book, and comes out the winner. He has killed the toughs. And the world, through the newspapers, make him "a national hero." But are he and Lacy content to end the book on that level? Hardly. Though cured of what he dreaded would be a cancerous growth in his bowels, and a national hero, Bond had seen the dark shadow of his being and could not stand the view: "I had seen Marty Bond a little too clearly these last few days, [and] I didn't want to live." And, he "lets go." It is a melodramatic ending, with an even more absurd stylistic conclusion, since the story is told in the first person, and Bond should have lived long enough to have written the story before dying. But no matter. It is really an interesting and revealing book about the early Ed Lacy.

Lacy developed his attitude and art into books which have a greater degree of honesty and realism, that tell about life as it pretty much is. These introduce a different and more satisfactory Lacy. Such a book is *Visa to Death* (1955). The plot is somewhat conventional, but there is a different basis of operations, a different dynamic working, and an improved outcome. The detective is a part-time dick and a full-time auto mechanic, and he prefers to be the mechanic. It is safer and steadier work. In this book he is approached by the ex-wife of a police officer who wants the detective to prove that her husband was not murdered but committed suicide. The plot turns around a group of people in New York City who are selling phony passports, killing when they have to in order to protect their business, and troubled at times with some honest hangers-on. Both sides of the detective's character drive him to be honest, to give an honest day's work for an honest day's pay. He doesn't want to play around with sex as payment.

This book states explicitly that one of Lacy's concerns is the need of the human being for human association and society. Throughout his books he deals with mentally deranged, socially excluded, lonely people who are deprived of the comfort of companionship. In the early *Men from the Boys* he had demonstrated that whites are often alienated from blacks and as a result mistreat them: Marty Bond, the seedy detective, though he has a loved black whore working for him, when he goes to Harlem to see her he refers to her kind of people as "you people," and she objects: " 'What you mean by *you* people? Aren't you people, Mr. Bond, a human being?' " And this "lip," as he calls it, annoys him back into recognizing the need of people for one another. This theme will continue, often with varying degrees applied to ethnic groups, and Blacks, to develop until it becomes a main theme.

Lacy, however, is a more satisfactory writer when he has a less conventional story to tell, when he manages to get outside the personal, private world of the private detective and takes on larger issues. To a certain extent such a study is *Sleep in Thunder* (1964). This story is about a poor Puerto Rican boy (and Puerto Ricans in general in New York City) named Jose who has to work after school as a delivery boy for a grocery store. Jose is set up by a hoodlum who steals sixty thousand dollars from an armored car and then plants two-hundred-dollar-bills on Jose to see if the whole loot can be safely spent. One of the two hoods who heisted the sixty thousand is named Sun, the other Lefty. Sun double-crosses Lefty and tries to keep the sixty thousand for himself. Lefty, however, kills Sun and nearly kills Jose. Jose becomes a hero to himself, the police force and his family. This story, though melodramatic, is lively and realistic.

It represents a concern that evidences itself to one degree or another throughout Lacy's works. Like E.V. Cunningham's concern for Mexicans in Beverly Hills, Lacy worried about the weak and vulnerable—always women, ethnic groups, and Blacks. In *Visa to Death* he had written with disgust about how New York City police tied up a Puerto Rican boy and simply beat him each time a cop passed by him.

Another example of his wider range is *The Napalm Bugle* (1968). This is a story about international intrigue, disillusioned war heroes and world destruction. Brad, the hero, is a Medal of Honor veteran and the editor of *The Napalm Bugle*, a strongly anti-war paper. He edits it because he feels strongly that his cause is just. The evil that was Korea is even more evident here:

> General, there's so much bullshit in the world I try to keep my head above it and not add any. The world is full of frauds and I think the worst fraud is the cold war. The fear of the atomic bomb, whether folks realize it or not, is the cause of our to hell-with-everything atmosphere, the lack of any sense of social responsibility. A man can only be happy living an honest life; hence I concentrate on espousing the war fraud, which as I said, is the bullshit core (p. 2).

Nevertheless, for his own reasons, Brad is inveigled into working for the General and trying to root out aliens who are working against the best interests of the U.S. After many adventures in this country and out, Brad locates the aliens and destroys them. But the ending is somewhat ambiguous. Lacy for many books involved parallel developments, one story line told in italicized print before the regular roman-type face story. Sometimes the development is close, other times it seems to be widely tangential. In this particular story, the parallel development is close and tells the story on two different psychological levels. The book is framed in the italics, the story is told in the first person by a psycho who is in a mental institution because of what he did, or he did what he did because he was ready for a mental institution. In this development the story is interesting. Lacy's skill in telling both in such a way that each amplified the other is strong. It is a strong story.

As strong as these types of books are, however, and some are indeed meritorious, Lacy is by far his strongest when depicting black detectives dealing with whites in their own society or with blacks in black society. Lacy's relationship with blacks is interesting and had a profound effect on his writing. He was white himself, but married a black woman and had many black friends. This seems to have strongly influenced his attitude toward them as a group. In fact, Lacy is strongest in style and in feeling when he is writing about black women. It is almost as though somehow the influence of his wife permeated his personality and psyche and directed his pen. Through the books Lacy's feeling intensified. In the earlier books his attitude seemed ambivalent. In *The Men From the Boys*, for example, Lacy has several slurs about Negroes, one or two said by Marty Bond, his anti-hero. In *Sin in Their Blood*, blacks are called Niggers, though the statement is voiced by hated characters.

But in those books which center around blacks as heroes, and with them Lacy first began to swing from his anti-hero stance into positive treatment of heroes, Lacy is simply at his most humanistic philosophy and more meritorious writing.

Room to Swing (1957) details the adventures of a black detective who gets mixed up with TV people on Madison Avenue. He thinks he has been framed for murder, but actually hasn't. He is not a conventional hero. On the contrary he is much stronger, the writing much better. The leading black has the unlikely name Touissaint Moore but he is bigger and more intense than life. In order to try to clear his name he has to drive out to southern Ohio to investigate some whites. The town he has to visit is not favorable to blacks, especially when they start playing around with white women or asking about them, even the white prostitutes. Touie knows he is in forbidden territory, he remembers his father's counsel: "A Negro's life is dirt cheap because he hasn't any rights a white man must respect. That's the law, the Dred Scott Decision, son. Always remember that." And Moore knows that he has taken his life into his own hands by being seen nosing around southern Ohio. As he remarks "As somebody once said, there are more horses' asses than horses in the world, and at the moment I felt like the number-one rear. I'd been crazy driving fifteen hours to this hayseed town where I stuck out like a sore thumb. Still, I was here and maybe the answer was, too." (p. 9) The answer is there, of course, and Moore discovers it and proves his own innocence.

Lacy's writing here is firm, fiery, realistic. The reader sweats through the hot days and nights as Moore confronts bigotry and hatred. The reader is made nervous by being with Moore on the fine line he must straddle between success and death. And the reader is jubilant in experiencing Moore's ultimate victory. The story and the style are reminiscent of John Ball's story on the same subject, *In the Heat of the Night.*

In *Room to Swing*, Moore's girl friend wants him to resign as a detective and become a mail-carrier. So to please her he resigns and turns to this safer job. It is hard to understand what this symbolizes unless Lacy is trying to point out that Blacks are by nature timid and retiring, wanting security and safety, until pushed into violence by society and events.

Anyway, in *Moment of Untruth* (1967), Lacy's second book featuring Moore, Touie is a mail-carrier, but is called back into being a private eye by his friends at the TV company. This time he must go to Mexico to investigate a murder. Here the race relations of white vs. black is played out against a different background, and with somewhat different results. The white woman he goes down to see is a university professor investigating anti-venom derived from snakes' venom. The murderer is a cowardly bull-fighter who has been weakening his bulls by injecting them with South American poison so that he can overcome them and be the great hero. He always takes the heart and liver of the slain bull and destroys them so that his adoring public won't know that the bull has been poisoned; they get the rest of the bull to eat themselves. Touie is the real hero, having solved the crime; the phony bull-fighter, though touted as a hero, is in fact a coward.

Two other books by Lacy treat black heroes and the race relations of the sixties. *Harlem Underground* (1965) is about the long hot summers of the 60s. Lee Hayes, a black detective who wants to make lieutenant, is sent disguised into Harlem to ferret out a gang of terrorists who are threatening an upcoming event. He moves into the house of a family, a punk male and two girls. Although his background is that of downtown police, Lee recognizes the justice of the Blacks' unrest and resentment. He is tempted to join them in their protest, and does voice their injustice that he himself feels. His white helper, a woman named Mary, is killed by Purple Eyes, the leader of the terrorist group. But Lee tells the blacks that he is interested in humanity, that all people though superficially different, must fight for the future and improvement of the human race. At the end he discovers Purple Eyes, who is the "janitor" custodian and owner of the house he has been living in. Turned back into the cop he is, and guaranteed to make lieutenant, Lee is, as several people say, the "hero." But he is not sure of his position. He argues with his cop pal, Jack, about the justice of the Blacks' demands, and how Whites must realize that justice and join in improving society. Jack thinks that things are much better than they used to be and will continue to improve. Lee, with his experience, doubts it, and insists that changes must be made or the summers will continue to be long and hot.

This is indeed a powerful book, gripping; the setting and development are authentic, the language realistic. It is surely one of Lacy's two or three most powerful books.

So too is *In Black & Whitey* (1967), which is typical of the many novels of the sixties dealing with how the city (that is urban life) is about to be torched by rebelling Blacks. Hugh Pentecost wrote two or three powerful novels on the subject, as did many others. In Lacy's book this time, the setting is Paradise Alley in Harlem, the characters are poor, underworked Blacks, who are ripe for riot. The neighborhood is being aggravated by a white group called WON, Wipe Out Negroes. A black and a white (Jewish) detective go under cover into Paradise Alley to see what is causing all the trouble and to rout the troublemakers. They of course succeed in discovering the WON monsters just before the city goes up in flames, and for the time being the torch is cooled.

The book is fascinating, filled with action and living people. The language is hip but authentic. Lacy knows his city people, especially his Blacks. There is cynical talk of heroes. Cops will be heroes for a day, leaders of the blacks will be the dead genuine heroes.

These books on Black-White relations actually touch on and develop the main thrust of Lacy's philosophy, and feelings. These cover two large areas: the development and role of the hero and, branching out, the value of humanity and compassion in society.

In developing his hero, Lacy actually swings about 180 degrees from the anti-hero of his first books, such people as Marty Bond of *Visa to Death* and Matt in *Sin in Their Blood*. In swinging to full hero, Lacy uses as his fulcrum "mythical" American patriots. In *Sleep in Thunder*, the white local cop, Paul Stein, is promoted for his work in helping the Puerto Rican boy trap the robbers, but the hero somehow turns out to be Benjamin Franklin; a quote from whom provides the title of the book and somehow the moral: "A quiet conscience sleeps in thunder." In *Room to Swing*, although Touissaint is the nominal hero, somehow Thomas Jefferson is the godfather if not the hero. He provides the clinching quote of the book: "The mass of mankind has not been born with saddles on their backs, nor a favored few booted and spurred..." From these mythical figures, who provide a philosophical basis for Lacy's works, the line of heroes develops through the Blacks who lay their lives on the line to protect the society which excludes them from all their rights in it.

Philosophically, Lacy has come from a rather neutral stance on the rights of individuals, though clearly on the side of what most people think is "right," to strong and powerful statements about what the Constitution of the United states guarantees and American society cannot get along without. The later books bristle with statements of the need for humanity and understanding and empathy. Like so many other authors who were writing during this period and later (Hugh Pentecost, John Ball, E.V. Cunningham), Lacy lays open the wound of society in its palpitating danger and invites all curious eyes to examine the body before it becomes a corpse.

In so doing, although some of the early books are conventional, the likes of which we have read often, the later ones are about as powerful in their statements and attitudes as one will find. And Lacy, at his best, is as profitable as the most readable.

E.V. Cunningham:
The Case of the Poisoned Society

With this author, the pendulum from the naked violence of Judson Philips and Ed Lacy has swung far to the other extreme. There is not the split-knuckle action here that characterizes the other authors. There is, also, a great distance between this author, who centers on the urban jungle that Arthur Upfield never touched, and those works about rural Australia. But there is one great similarity between Cunningham and Upfield: both have been concerned with the whole spectrum of the world they inhabit, with the various kinds of people, their motivations, their actions. Cunningham does not achieve the explosive power of Philips, Lacy or Upfield, but with the last-named author, he shares comprehensiveness.

E.V. Cunningham (Howard Fast 1919-   ), who has also written under the name of Walter Ericson, is an author of many attitudes and approaches to his basic philosophy: that the world is evil because people have departed from humanity but that there is ultimate triumph of the common person. Cunningham is an experimental author who probes reality in various ways, who happened to choose crime fiction because as he said, these books "were far more fun to write than serious novels." In nearly all his works he is, with varying degrees, almost always successful.

His first crime series, beginning with a book named *Sylvia* (1958) ran for eleven books in what Frank Campenni calls "high-heeled thrillers." These use the single name of a woman as the title, *Sylvia*, *Alice, Shirley, Helen*, etc., and in so doing tend to throw the books into mythology (Calypso, Ruth, Circe, Medusa). Cunningham pictures the rather unusual (at times problematical) day-to-day activities of women to show that the female world in America is insecure, vulnerable, uneasy, but that the average woman is able to handle herself and fend off danger. Written in the sixties these books helped in the fight for women's rights, for they are strong statements in Cunningham's apparent belief that of the two sexes, woman is the stronger.

Except, of course, the women, though pictured as ordinary housewives, as prostitutes, etc., are not run-of-the-mill people, and their world is hardly everyday. They are quite unusual ordinary women living in a world run amok.

Alice (1963), for example, is a thriller which takes the ordinary life of a New York suburban family and turns it into unmitigated terror. One afternoon on the subway platform as he is heading home, Johnny, the husband, is approached by a stranger who slips a key into his pocket unbeknownst and then jumps (or is pushed) under the subway train. The key is to a locker in the city filled with a valuable commodity, but Johnny, not knowing that the key is in his pocket, cannot respond affirmatively when the mob contacts him and asks for it. Consequently his wife, Alice, and their children get involved and become objects of terrorism. The book is well written, suspenseful, filled with real life characters, and is apparently designed to show that not only is the female the superior of the sexes but that a woman is superior to terrorism also. It is a thoroughly readable book.

Shirley (1964) is an absolute delight. Again an entirely different kind of book, Cunningham is experimenting with a cool, hip, laid-back female character, a beautiful secretary from the Bronx. She is a literary version of the TV personality Rhoda Morgenstern, but with more life and more wit. She may be a little typecast, and she may sound like a very caricature of the Bronx broad, but Shirley has life, individuality. She has more wit in a paragraph than most people have in an entire book. The work is thoroughly delightful.

Helen (1966) is a different kind of book, and is both a success and failure because it attempts a great deal and somehow does not bring it all off. Helen is a newly arrived lady in San Verdo (Las Vegas), where as a seeming prostitute she gets to know men of wealth and power. One of them is murdered, and Helen is accused of the crime; she is either being railroaded or is guilty. A naive, idealistic lawyer, Blake Eddyman (a thin disguise for Everyman), has the defense of Helen forced upon him by the District Attorney. Blake is mesmerized by Helen's beauty and mysteriousness, so much that he gives up his charming wife just to be ignored and cursed by Helen. Helen, for her part, is a surrealistic character, dark, sultry, enigmatic, evasive and not as bright and well developed as she might have been. As the age-old dark lady of mystery and evil, she is indifferent to her own fate, and is willing to drag others down with her fall. Helen (of Troy. At her end, her face looks like "an old piece of Greek sculpture") voices one side of Cunningham's question about humanity.

She is fatalistic. To her "evil, sin, bad" are meaningless words, because the world is "warped—a whole world" (p. 140). But Cunningham's philosophy counters her gloomy picture. He believes that love in fellow human beings and humanitarianism are the answers to loneliness and destruction.

Penelope (1965) is a woman of a different dress altogether. A light put-on, a spoof comedy about a woman who is so bored and flappy that she takes up robbing her husband's bank as a bit of fun. And she gets away with it, as Cunningham does. This book is a tight rubber band in C sharp minor.

Samantha (1967 re-published as *The Case of the Angry Actress*), the second in the single name series, began the *The Case of...* series of four books, which use Masao Masuto as the detective and which shift Cunningham's approach from woman to the whole of society. In this series Cunningham is not concerned with the strength of women but with the split between the worlds of the wealthy and powerful and the poor and the weak. He chooses Beverly Hills as the center of the rich and evil, surrounded by the poor, everyday world of Los Angeles, with its superior people.

The Case of the Three-Penny Orange (1977), one of the early books under this series of titles, is a stronger, more developed book.

The contrast between Beverly Hills and Los Angeles is set early in the book: "Masao Masuto lived in Culver City, and for those unfamiliar with the geography of Los Angeles it may be said that while Culver City is only a few minutes by car from Beverly Hills, by property values and popularization it is a continent away" (p. 29). Because he is "of a curious disposition" "Beverly Hills provoked him to endless curiosity," but Masuto really is concerned with the larger picture, with those people who care for others.

Living in the two worlds of his daily existence, Masuto is keenly aware that his is a complex society, but so is everyone's. His task is to find some simple way into his own life style. If that at times seems to make him appear to possess a complex mind, that is only another of the complexities of society: "Accused of having a complex mind, Masuto would protest that his manner of thinking and being was simple and direct. He was aware that he lived in perhaps the most complex society that the world had ever evolved; his problem was always to find some simple and direct path through the complexity" (*Orange*, p. 108).

A part of his problem of being a policeman, especially in Beverly Hills, is the fact that Masuto is a Nisei, that is an American born of Japanese parents. In California, where there are so many Japanese and Niseis, Masuto feels that perhaps people should recognize his kind. Yet, generally despised by the people of the city, and humorously kidded by his few colleagues on the small police force, Masuto is called a "Jap" at least half a dozen times in every book, and is mistaken for Chinese, and every other kind of Oriental that the ignorant people around him can imagine. Yet Masuto is patient; his answer to every slur is almost stock; he explains his heritage very carefully, and generally to everyone's satisfaction. But having to explain himself and justify his existence, as it were, makes Masuto keenly aware of other "oppressed" minorities in the LA area, especially Mexicans, and particularly Mexican women and children. Frequently such people are indifferently killed by the wealthy, or are deliberately used, exploited and murdered after they are no longer useful. For example, in *The Case of the Poisoned Eclairs* (1979) a Mexican housekeeper of a wealthy family is inadvertently, even carelessly, killed when a plot to kill a rich lady goes astray. But no matter to the wealthy; her death generates hostility in Masuto's heart though professionally he must solve the murder coolly and dispassionately.

Another story involving roughly the same kinds of people inflames Cunningham's indignation. *The Case of the Sliding Pool* (1981) revolves around a skeleton that becomes exposed when a Malibu swimming pool slides down a hill after heavy rains and reveals a skeleton that obviously had been placed there just before the concrete had been poured. As it turns out, a contractor had been guilty of the crime, and this time the guilt sprays over onto a rich and haughty Japanese relative of Masuto.

In developing this story, Cunningham uses as his motivation the fate of the poor and weak. The corpse is obviously that of a working man. In this book, as in others, there is a Mexican housemaid, Rosita, who is being sought to be murdered only because she is weak. Masuto flares with hatred. Crime against anyone is intolerable: "Crime encapsulated the general illness of mankind" (p. 4) and criminals "have surrendered all claim to being a part of the human race" (p. 142). This time, though still a Zen Buddhist and therefore concerned with humanity though peacefully as much as possible, and though he usually could "look at the enormous wealth and very conspicuous consumption of Beverly Hills with objectivity and without envy" and though he is awed by the wealth of one of his in-laws, Masuto classes all criminals together, and condemns them.

The main trouble with the world, as Masuto and Cunningham see it, is violence. People kill one another carelessly, indifferently, mainly for personal gain, to cover up past mistakes, but sometimes merely because they have forgotten themselves. In *The Case of the Three-Penny Orange*, Masuto tells his police chief that "Violence is the disease of our times." In answer to the inquiry by his wife, Kati, why men commit murder, Masuto's response reflects his general worry about the human race: "Because they lose themselves somewhere and in that way they lose the rest of mankind."

Generally the culprits are run-of-the-mill WASPS. Cunningham has a great respect for Japanese other than the Nisei Masuto. They seem to constitute a minority enclave that are oppressed and should stick together. They have great respect for one another, for their traditions. Masuto has many wealthy in-laws through his wife, and has a special downtown LA Buddhist monk whom he visits when he needs to find peace of mind or assistance in putting together some especially tough purpose in human activity. Yet even the inscrutable and peaceful Japanese can depart from their training and break the law. Cunningham's final outlook is bound to be gloomy. Even the Japanese lose the rest of mankind.

It is this fragmentation, the dissolution of the bonds of mankind that plagues Masuto, tearing his heart out with worry and anxiety, making him toil to solve his murder problems in unusually brief periods, usually because of the peculiar conditions of life style and desires in "peaceful" Beverly Hills.

In resolving the murders he charts the distance people have departed from the common bonds they should have as human beings. In getting the cooperation of people who are not guilty, he reminds them that they ought to help him because "they are members of the human race." That is they have more in common with other people, and a greater debt to the good members of the human race, than they have with the people who, for their own reasons, set out to destroy the human race, or at least portions of it.

Masuto is something of a hero in the eyes of his police chief, Wainwright, and with the other members of the small Beverly Hills police force; the captain often claims that Masuto is one of the best homicide detectives in the business. He especially likes to say this to members of the CIA or FBI or the other smart alec bureaucrats from the East. Berkman, Masuto's work partner, thinks he is effective, and although the other cops in the LA district cities give him a hard time they cooperate and assist Masuto in solving his crimes.

But Masuto is most heroic in the eyes of the women in the books. At first the women, like all other people in LA and Beverly Hills, are nonplused at the thought of a Japanese being on the police force of Beverly Hills. How did he get on it, is he—small of stature, etc.— capable of handling their problems? Should they answer his questions, pay him any attention, do what he requests? Can they safely tell him to "go to hell" and get out their houses

But Masuto charms them all. Soft-spoken, except when he gets heated up with righteous indignation, quite willing to slip into the "Ah So" stereotype of the Japanese, Masuto impresses them all with his thoroughness, his powers of observation, deduction, and his general charm. By the end of the books, his personality has worked miracles. The women who before had despised him, are telling him, "You know you are unusual, of course you know that" and are asking if he is married, apparently wanting to go to bed with him on a temporary or long-term basis, and generally treat the man for the hero that he really is. Masuto, however, is unusually heroic enough to resist all the sexual advances. His answers to all the promises of seduction and joy are that he is happily married and will have nothing to do with any woman but Kati, his wife. Not that Kati is perfect, as he admits. She worries too much, she is not the perfect Japanese wife that he would like (he often teases her that she is getting liberated and he should have married a more conventional Japanese woman but he in fact does not get bothered over the fact that she wants to read Betty Friedan and get "liberated"). And Masuto has a gentle and pleasant sense of humor and teasing which makes him a splendid companion in any group.

So far Cunningham has eight books in this series. Though individually successful, they become increasingly complex, as the author becomes more and more familiar with his detective, his environment and with what he wants to say. He is, however, still experimenting. In one, for example, *The Case of the Russian Diplomat* (1978), he reaches back to *Penelope* and gives us something of a spoof. The story reaches out into cliched surroundings and people with a Russian Diplomat and an Iranian terrorist group. The situation and the characters are not spoofs, but Cunningham has his formulas and cliches down so securely, his stereotypes so snug that he can write with a sense of detachment and pleasure that makes the book literally throb and smile at you.

A somewhat less successful book is one of his latest, *The Case of the Murdered Mackenzie* (1984). The cracks that were showing in the earlier effort at bringing in foreigners widen in this story. In some ways this is the most intense of Cunningham's works. A man presumably named Mackenzie is found dead and naked in a bathtub by his wife, all his clothes are missing, obviously very carefully removed and destroyed. The wife remarks, when viewing the corpse, "That is not my husband!" She is assumed to be the murderess, but is cleared. The explanation is, of course, that the corpse is the twin brother of the lady's husband, who is away and doing well. The story is hot to the touch, but is phony. The FBI and CIA are assumed to be in on the story, but as it turns out it is the KGB and other Russians who are out to get Mackenzie because he has turned traitor on them, and has lived with one of their most effective and beautiful spies, who is killed in the end. The ending is obviously a make-do conclusion taking advantage of the interest these days in international espionage, but the ending is not satisfactory. And this is not one of Cunningham's most successful endeavors.

In his latest effort, *The Wabash Factor* (1986), Cunningham takes another turn in his probing of detective and thriller fiction, though into a genre that is red-hot today—the terror novel. He creates a tough New York detective named Harry Golding and his firm-minded and outspoken Irish wife, Fran. There is a spate of murders made to look like natural though accidental deaths, such as heart attacks in restaurants, falling mortar and automobile accidents. As soon as Golding gets involved, somebody begins terrorizing his family and he has to send his children off to Ireland for safety. Golding and his wife investigate in New York City and Los Angeles and finally discover that the murders and reign of terror are mob-induced.

This novel is different in style as well as content from Cunningham's other works. In it his language is direct, vernacular and hard, though not crisp and electric. Cunningham manages to tighten the line of tension until the reader is really interested and involved, though it is a book that the reader can put aside for a while. The book suffers also because it is somewhat of a disappointment that Masuto, the Beverly Hills detective, is not in it. The prose style is tighter than that of the Masuto novels, but the book is not as interesting. It is unfortunate also that the book does not contain any of Cunningham's cultural and humanistic bias of the Masuto novels. Here Golding is a cop, his wife helps in his investigations. That is about all. Though interesting, the book does not really improve the stature of its author.

E. V. Cunningham is not a major writer of crime fiction for several reasons. First, his style is not hard-boiled enough to make him one of the major stylists in that genre. His characters are not quite important enough to make him a major social critic. Somehow Beverly Hills remains small and unimportant, not the equivalent of New York or Los Angeles, no matter how hard Cunningham tries to make it a microcosm of the world. Masuto is not fleshed out sufficiently to make him the universal living, breathing cop. He is a kind of Japanese-American Everyman, but is not inked in strongly enough to be both or either. He is a person in fiction whom you file away in the drawer of second importance. Yet Cunningham's message which he shares with Arthur Upfield, is universal, is timeless and of the utmost importance: we all belong to the same human race and elitists and everyday people should remember this. All in all, Cunningham writes interesting and worthwhile fiction. He is definitely on the should-read list.

The Chicago Talk of
Thomas B. Dewey

It is a long jump from the authors we have been discussing before
to the earlier author Thomas B. Dewey. There is clearly a leap in
both geography and time. In American geography the move is from
the American east and west coast (with trips outside the States) to
the Middle-West. In time the move is from the contemporary to an
earlier day, when detective writers were mistakenly called hard-boiled.
Like all catch phrases the term stuck, and has been used ever since
to designate a species of writers whose language was vernacular and
rough, whose guns and fists were often overly active, but whose hearts
were soft. The one trait that characterized all those so-called hard-
boiled writers was their soft, humanitarian hearts. They worked and
fought hard for the underdog, for the underprivileged, for those persons
that society, humanity—the world—had abused and knocked about.
The knights who took up their causes were driven by the knowledge
that there but for the grace of God or the Devil, walked themselves;
and they did not care to endorse the actions of society that were so
manifestly unfair. Besides, howl and lament their fate as they might,
these knights out to right wrongs enjoyed the fray. Few excelled in
their feats, their attitudes, or in the style of their chronicler the
characters and writings of this particular author whose beat was
Chicago and the Mid-West.

A much too neglected writer of genuine merit is Thomas B. Dewey,
author of at least 37 novels plus a handful of uncollected short stories,
and three other books. Writing at a time when he inevitably was
compared with the hard-boiled school of Hammett, Chandler and Ross
Macdonald, Dewey was acknowledged a craftsman whose characters
bled real blood on the streets of his world. But he tended to live in
the shadow of these perhaps superior writers, and as a result never
achieved the reputation and readership he deserved. Most of his works
have long been out of print. But now they are being reprinted at
least in part (by Carroll and Graf, New York) and those of us who
enjoy American detective stories in one of their major traditions can

once again have access to the fine stories and the splendid telling
that Dewey represents.

Dewey differs from the other writers about dicks on the mean
streets of American by not having heroes at all. Dewey's characters
include an honest District Attorney, an avenging cop and a Los Angeles
private eye. All have their problems, but are not genuinely unusual.
In one novel, however, one private eye was unusual to the point of
being eccentric—and genuinely funny.

As *Good As Dead* (1948) is about the countryside around Gary,
Indiana, close to the Chicago and the countryside that Dewey wrote
about most. In this story, the brains of the detective work is a man
named Singer Batts, one of the most reluctant detectives who ever
tracked down criminals. He is by habit a small-town scholar,
bibliophile and reader who does not like having his reading interrupted
and often will not pay attention to anything said or done to him
before he has finished a chapter in a book because he "can't stop
in the middle of a marginal note." Yet when on the trail of criminals
Batts is witty, clever and unrelenting as well as slothful. As is his
harder-nosed helper, the manager of a small hotel, Joe Spinder. In
this story, a certain woman presumably returns to her home town
after some twenty years and takes up residence in her father's old
house on the edge of town. She is murdered, and thus sets off a string
of events which embroils most of the curious people of the town and
especially those who like to dig into mysteries.

Throughout his career, Dewey wrote of people in the mean country
and on the streets of the cities who were not heroic at all. They are
almost like the rest of us, somewhat indifferent to the fate of others,
somewhat lazy, slothful, and leaning a little more than 180 degrees
south of the upright when facing north. These characteristics will
continue to develop in Dewey's fiction through the years. But it has
a splendid beginning in this early work. The writing is fanciful—
even playful—but altogether serious in intent. Take as a good example
this passage from *As Good As Dead* (p. 111):

> Singer was lying on the floor a little way off. He looked dead. He looked
> so dead that I started to cry and I broke away from one of the guys and kicked
> him in the groin. He sat down on the floor. The other one hit me in the face
> and I hit back at him, missed, lost my balance and fell down. He picked me
> up and I kicked him in the belly. He sat down. But by this time the other one
> was up and I couldn't win. He got me pinned against the table. Gorilla lifted
> his gun and hit me in the face with it. It struck the bridge of my nose and I

gave up. I just stood there, feeling the pain and the rage and the fact that Singer was lying there and altogether it was the worst moment of my life.

In fact Singer is almost as much a comic figure as a serious one. Joe always has to take care of him. But he did this gladly because Singer had "done a lot" for Joe and the only way he could repay him was by looking after Singer's best interests. Sometimes this caretaking became a bit intrusive. For example, at the very end of the book, when the mystery of the hanging woman had been solved and Joe is about to make time in the car with his girl friend, who should stick his befuddled face from the rear seat but Batts:

"There was a sound in the back seat. Automatically my hand jumped to my coat pocket. I looked around slowly.
   Climbing up from the floor to the back seat was my ever-loving Singer Batts. He got on the seat and looked at me foolishly.
   I just looked. I couldn't say anything.
   " 'Well—' Singer said at last, "you've been telling me I couldn't get a bride by correspondence. I thought'—
   " 'Yeah?' I said, as his voice dwindled away.
   " 'I thought I would just come along for a first-hand lesson in wooing.'
   I looked down at Genevieve. She was laughing.
   " 'Don't make him walk back to town, darling,' she said.
   I kissed her.

   These early detectives although marked exclusively with Dewey's brand, were conventional in having names. In fact Dewey was excellent with names: for example one of the meanies in this book is named simply "Gorilla". But his greatest skill with names brought him finally to the realization that if names are significant, ("Dingo" in *Portrait of a Dead Heiress*), the lack of names is perhaps even more significant. Early in his career he discovered that he wanted his main detective throughout most of his books to be named simply "Mac." This is the most democratic name in America. No surname, nothing distinctive about the given name. Just the object of every person's call: "Hey, Mac." Characterless, undistinguished from everybody else. The voice of democracy.
   Another of Dewey's variations from the non-heroic tradition and from the "Mac" as detective tradition is *Hunter at Large* (1961). This time a police detective named Mickey Phillips, is beaten up and forced to watch while his dearly beloved wife is murdered before his eyes. The Captain fears that Mickey will be unable to free his obsession with catching the killers, and therefore grants Mickey a two-year leave of absence. During those two years Mickey has various adventures

in the west and especially in Mexico, but eventually runs down the
two men responsible for his wife's death and liquidates them. Then
he is able to come back to the police force. Not necessarily a trend-
setter in vigilante fiction, this story is as tight, compelling and moving
as any. Dewey has his language vernacular, his psychology sufficiently
off-balance, and his story unrelenting: His style is as compelling as
any other's in the business:

Mickey aimed carefully and shot Teller low in the belly. The big man buckled,
fell forward, rolled onto the grass. Wister was coming at him across the hood
of the car, scrambling. There was a knife in his hand. Mickey, blocked now by
the open car door, backed off to get in the clear. Wister slid over the hood, grabbed
the door for support and managed to get his balance. He formed a target
momentarily, then, as Mickey aimed to shoot, he dived at Mickey's ankles, slashed
upward with his knife.

Mickey fell hard in the street. He rolled to keep his head from striking the
concrete and felt the knife blade deep in his thigh, a red-hot pain. Wister was
clawing his way up over his legs. Mickey twisted desperately, clubbed at the other's
head. The blow glanced off to Wister's shoulder and he was still coming. The
knife was up in Wister's right hand. Mickey dropped the gun, caught Wister's
forearm in both hands and swung it up in a long arc against the normal articulation
of the ball-and-socket. Wister screamed with pain and rolled away. The knife
clattered wetly on the pavement. Mickey reached the car, pulled himself up and
stood against the fender, sucking air in huge gasps... (p. 183).

In *Call me Mac*, almost as prophetic as Melville's beginning of
Moby-Dick, "Call me Ishmael," there is a society that is becoming
more and more democratic in its violence. "Mac" works hard to
maintain his anonymity. When he has to give his name, as in some
public place, he simply writes it down but we are not informed of
it. When he has to give a name as over a telephone, he says simply
"I gave him my name." Dewey deliberately obscures the surname of
his detective so that we can never see beyond the democratic moniker
"Mac." (The only other person in detective fiction who has recognized
the heroic proportions in the use of names seems to be Bill Pronzini,
who simply because he could not decide on a name for his main
character discovered that he really liked for the person to be "nameless,"
and has kept him that way ever since the first accidental discovery.)

Dewey follows through with this name-device regardless of where
his stories take him, from the Midwest to the West-Coast, in cars,
on trains and in various other means of travel.

In *Every Bet's A Sure Thing* (1953), Mac is hired by a Chicago
agency to see somebody to the West Coast on the train because it
is assumed that the woman is under surveillance from other sources.

Mac reluctantly accepts the job, throws himself together and makes the train. Halfway out, he is caught by the person who is surveilling the woman, is thrown off the train and abandoned. But, exhibiting the skill and innovativeness of the truly skilled detective, Mac hires an airplane to fly him to Las Vegas, where he again catches the same train and recommences his surveillance. Finally, in Los Angeles, from the beaches inward, Mac solves the problem of why the woman was being surveilled and eventually murdered.

But the story is more than it seems. There are woven into the fabric at least two of the themes that obsessed Dewey's writing. There is, as mentioned, the non-heroic hero Mac, the man who although often kicked and mugged, perseveres and survives. There is also another theme that permeates Dewey's fiction almost throughout, his concern with the weak and vulnerable in this world, especially women and children. Though beautiful women throw themselves naked into his arms, Mac is less interested in them than in the social well-being. And, like Ross Macdonald alongside and after him, Dewey is interested in the vulnerable and fatherless child. The question nearly always with him is: "Who will take care of the children?" Since the children seldom have advocates, Mac takes the task upon himself.

Generally the children are vulnerable and need protection. But not always. In *The Mean Streets* (1954), they do not. Every kid from the age of eight up is in some kind of racket, picking pockets, mugging, murdering, being accessories before and after the fact. Mac is the baseball coach, and interested in why one of the kids is no longer coming to school. In order to conceal the dark side of their lives, kids kill and kids are killed. But throughout Mac is on their side, moving among them and trying to save or salvage them from themselves. The story is an excellent example of how Dewey can write on one of his favorite subjects and treat it in a manner that is from the other side of his desires. It represents a writer in control of his emotions and his skills.

When Dewey walks the corridors or the streets of Chicago he is as effective as any street-watcher in the business. Perhaps one of his best examples is *Portrait of a Dead Heiress* (1967). In this story, a young heiress winds up in a bathtub filled with water, apparently a suicide because of depression. But Mac knows that things smell fishy if not oceany. He traces his way through the lady's past, discovers unsavory acts and people, and eventually brings to justice the guilty party. In so doing, Dewey in his prose style imitates nature so much that the book is both obsessive and terrifying. In a funeral scheme, for example, Dewey's words are as rhythmic as the strokes of death:

It didn't take long. An organ played some slow music. A man in a black suit said a few words of comfort and commended the soul of Lorrie King to heaven and the organ played again and that was all. Everybody sat still and waited while Lorrie's mother and family rose and left the chapel. And I sat and waited while Dr. Kramm went out, then Saunders and finally Dillion.

In any of a dozen books, Dewey is at his absolute best, and not far short of the most effective writers of detective fiction. Generally his prose does not sing with the poetry of Raymond Chandler's nor the turgid emotion of Dashiell Hammett's, or the tenderness of Ross Macdonald's. But his prose is tense, vernacular, dramatic and compelling. At its strongest, the plots are as tense as fine-strung wire, the emotion as unrelenting as approaching crisis.

Deadline (1966) is perhaps as good an example of the qualities an any other. A twenty-two year old young man is four days away from the electric chair, having been convicted of rape and murder. Mac is hired by some people who think the young man is innocent, or at least his life should be spared, to uncover new evidence. He goes to the small town to talk with the people. There he discovers not sympathy and assistance, but hostility and stonewalling. Blocked and frustrated at every turn, Mac, unheroically, calls his lawyer-employer in Chicago every day asking for instructions and reporting his failure. But though slow, Mac is persevering. Based on a chance remark, he discovers new leads, successfully faces down members of the town and saves the boy's life.

The writing is Dewey at his strongest. The books opens with one of his strongest themes:

Peter Davidian was twenty-two years old. That's young to die. But Peter Davidian, barring a last-minute miracle, surely would die within a week. He would die the bad way, in a steel chair wired with enough voltage to light up a good-sized town, with his head shaved and his pants legs slit. They say you don't feel it, but at twenty-two I guess you feel it now and then while waiting.

Though hard-shelled and tough-sounding, the prose throbs with regret over young death and perhaps the thoughtless injustice of it all. Mac is a big man with a bigger heart.

At times, as in many of his other books, Dewey manages little vignettes of scenes that sparkle with delight. In one in this book, Mac is questioning the couple that Peter had lived with after his parents died. Mac questions the lady, while the husband "hovered like a tower" some distance away. He wanted to kibbitz the talk but not get involved himself. Yet he cannot resist. An except of the conversation goes like this:

> "Peter lived with you people, I understand,' I said.
> 'Yes, since he was twelve years old. He lost his parents, you see.'
> 'And you brought him up.'
> 'What kind of boy was he?'
> 'Oh, he was a good boy! Quiet and well-behaved—and work, my goodness.'
> Fred Sampson walked to a shelf, picked out a toothpick and began to pick his teeth.
> 'He was a hard worker,' he said unexpectedly.
> 'How did he do in school? I asked. Was he a pretty good student?'
> Mrs. Sampson looked somewhat embarrassed.
> 'Well—just average, I guess.'
> 'No good,' Fred Sampson said. He didn't care much for school. Couldn't seem to catch on good.'
> 'But he didn't fail,' Mrs. Sampson insisted.
> 'Kind of a dreamer,' Fred said. 'Always thinkin' about somethin' else.'
> I didn't want to take a chance on Mrs. Sampson's getting choked off and drying up on me, so I kept my attention on her.
> 'Was it a big shock to him, losing his parents?' I asked her. 'How did it happen?'
> 'A young boy like that,' she said, 'it was very hard. He was the only one. They had a farm down the road here and things didn't go too well for them— it was a poor farm—'
> 'Davidian was a poor farmer,' Fred put in. 'Drank. Didn't take to farmin'. You have to take to it.' "

The final denouement is carried on with such a breathlessness that it is unexcelled in detective fiction. Mac maneuvers to get the main contestants in a barn and in a car racing toward that barn, against a dawn deadline, and the events unfold verbally and physically with breath-taking speed. But naturally. Dewey's timing and rhythm are just right.

At the end of the drama, Mac plays his role to the hilt. Always a loner, always Mr. Nobody, he wins the battle but loses the larger war of love and companionship, fading away instead into the nameless background, waiting for another call to assist the needy. The books end thusly; teasingly, and unemotionally but unrelentingly:

The drama ended, Mac and his newly-found girl Caroline Adams are walking away from the final enactment:

> We stood there for a moment in the morning sun.

' "Parlez-vous francais?'I said.
'*Oui . . .*'
'*S'il vous plait*—have breakfast with me?'
She smiled.
'Any time,' she said. 'Any time at all, when you're free.'
I took her hand and we started up the street toward the Wesley Cafe.
'Do you speak French, really?' she said.
'No, uh-uh,' I said. 'No, I don't. I speak Chicago.'"
Her hand moved in mine as we started to cross the street. It was a good hand. She was a good girl. I never saw her again after that time in Wesley.

In such an ending, which is typical of Dewey's works, there is a forlornness, a sadness, a melancholy that almost breaks the spirit. The role of the white knight, the black knight, the nameless knight in society is one of loneliness, of being alone. Generally liaison between him and society breaks off after some interchange has been established and completed. Sometimes the contact is never completed, as in the ending of *Portrait of a Dead Heiress*, which ends with the melancholy lines, "The telephone rang again, once again, and stopped abruptly as the receiver went up at the other end." Society benefits and remains relatively healthy. Mac worries on, never too confident in his success, and desperately queasy in his failures, as he states in *Portrait of a Dead Heiress*: "I turned off the light and lay in the dark with the faint sickness you have when you've fluffed on a client." But unlike society, which sometimes breaks down and quits, Mac forges ahead; he is merely playing out his role. In *The King Killers* (p. 154) he says,"Don't have faith. Just keep moving." Unlike society he doesn't whine and quail; he fulfills his obligations, big with compassion and understanding, little with loneliness. The language that Dewey speaks, though clean, clear, sharp and communicative, is the voice of loneliness and sadness. His "Chicago" language is universal and timeless.

The Humanistic Eggs: Fiction of Michael Z. Lewin

Nowadays the growing interest of ethnicity and regionalism in everyday life exemplified by Thomas B. Dewey is increasingly being paralleled by a healthy growth in the sites and cities that detective fiction writers live in and write about. In addition to the major cities and crime areas—such as New York, Boston, Chicago, San Francisco, LA, Vegas—numerous writers are turning out quite interesting stories about the crime and private detectives in such cities as Detroit, Minneapolis, Madison, Omaha, Cincinnati and others including many small towns. They live in and write about these cities because the authors know their territories and feel them significant as subject-areas. As William J. Reynolds, in *The Nebraska Quotient* (1984) remarked, when asked why he chose Omaha as his subject-area: "It's not LA., New York, Boston, or any other glamorous place; I know the city; and there's something cowboy-ish about it, which appeals to my belief that the 'P.I.' is the modern variation of the cowboy myth. I called my P.I. Nebraska for the same reason—it's a very Western, very American word." There is of course a profound truth in Reynolds statement, despite the fact that there is a certain lack of originality about the observation that the P.I. is the modern variation of the cowboy myth. Reynolds' comment about the Americanness of Omaha, of his P.I. named Nebraska, and the value of writing about the surroundings that one knows best is of course valid and important. Such knowledge formed the backbone of the writers we have studied earlier.

One of the most interesting and far too little talked about is the author of a series of stories, Michael Z. Lewin, who grew up in Indianapolis, went to school at Harvard, now lives in Somerset, England and writes about a private investigator named Albert Samson who lives in and works out of Indianapolis.

Lewin is an unusual kind of American author of private investigator novels. Albert Samson, the P.I. is not hard-boiled; he's not even an egg boiled for any duration. He is instead like the eggs he often cooks himself for breakfast: scrambled, soft, scorched by failure around the edges and with a gentle pepper or two in the middle. He is anti-heroic, or non-heroic in the natural sense of the term.

Samson is a jack of all trades and failure in all. He is a photographer, carpenter, odd-jobber and P.I. He lives alone in an office-apartment that was given to him gratis by a former client who was grateful for a job he once did. Samson "dines" on hamburgers and other cheap food at Dan's Diner and goes home to his mother often, though not as often as she would like, because she understands how a man in his later 40s can be a failure in all things. He admits his poverty, which is extreme: even his bathrobe has holes in it, and his boxer shorts have patches on them.

Yet living in the ghetto himself, Samson hates violence and will avoid it through every conceivable avenue of evasion and cowardice when possible; he despises guns because he is afraid of them. He once shot a person, not dead but "just enough to kill something in me," as he said. About violence he remarked, "I am not a man of violence, and I am especially not a fan of violent death. It's too random as it is practiced in the modern world." (*The Way We Die Now*, 1971), (p. 17) Being known by all, especially the reader, as a believer in non-violence, Samson sometimes will develop his persona by pretending to be a man of great violence. In *Ask the Right Question* (1971), for example, in talking about a woman who is shot by another person, he puffs up like an Australian Frilled Lizard into the most awesome person of violence: "If I had been me I would have had that gun up and shot her full of holes. I swear I would, so help me...I lack a certain degree of self control. I would have made her into mincemeat." (p. 185-6)

In his style of writing, Lewin has not developed the formula that makes composition of P.I. novels easy and fits a book into the series of formula expectations the reader might like. Samson, the detective, is ever developing, not quite solidified, and is therefore changing subtly, growing, acting human. Thus all books are somewhat different from the others. Lewin seems to be writing and developing his character along lines that he likes rather than those he might assume the readers expect. In one book, *Hard Line* (1982), Lewin's main character is Lt. Leroy Powder, and Albert Samson gets merely a cameo one-paragraph appearance.

One of the interesting aspects of Lewin's writing is his use of literary material. A Harvard graduate and presumably therefore familiar with literature, he uses his literary references, in an unusual and refreshing way, not by quoting sections of poems and prose works and working off them or merely displaying his knowledge of them but by having them play through his mind and surface casually and naturally, as in everyday life. Samson went through college two times, once for a year and a half and once for one-half a year, so the references come naturally, sometimes as half-remembrances that he doesn't bother to correct. For example, in *Ask the Right Question* (1971), he alludes to both Wordsworth and Coleridge: "I stopped humming, aware for the third time that my consciousness was collapsing around me. Too much alone late and soon, not enough begetting and spending" (33) (*The World is Too Much With Us* and *The Rime of the Ancient Mariner*) After a hangover he says, he "woke up with fuzz in my face. Fuzz, fuzz everywhere, and not one with a peaches blush" (94). He seems to like the Romantic poets so much that he named the daughter of his lady-friend Lucy (after Wordsworth's Lucy poems). In *The Silent Salesman* Samson is leaped upon by a 190 pound body which is, like Hamlet's problem with morality, "too solid fresh" (234). In *The Way We Die Now* (1971) Samson goes into a lavish living room that brings up echoes of *Pride and Prejudice*: "Elizabeth Bennet would stand here; Fitzwilliam Darcy thus" (84).

Echoes of other kinds, sometimes obvious sometimes less so, fleet through his works. In *The Way We Die Now*, there is a man in a mental hospital who, separated from his home and family, cites the popular song "Irene" as his philosophy: "Go home to your wife and your family. Stay by your fireside bright." (Lewin says that the tune was "Irene.") In examining some pornographic photos, Samson makes perhaps the obvious literary reference to Andrew Marvell's poem "To His Coy Mistress," in how he would treat the situation "If there were time, my Coy Mistress." In *Ask the Right Question* he echoes the Harry James-Helen Forrest popular song of the 1940s, "They're Writing Songs of Love," by saying, "A siren howled. But not for me." (59) At times Samson's references are almost personal and arcane. For example in *The Silent Salesman* he does not make any reference to the fascinating Australian author of the Napoleon Bonaparte series, Arthur Upfield, but gives Upfield's favorite Australian affirmation: "Too right you will."

As in other ways, Lewis runs counter to the hard-boiled tradition in not being macho and chauvinistic. He treats women with respect and sympathy. In some ways, however, he seems uncomfortable, probably because he is an admitted failure, considers himself inferior, and therefore has to somehow compensate for his failings. He has

a "woman" in Indianapolis, who is always angry with him for
something he has not done, for his mooching food off her and for
not wanting to get married. We occasionally go with Samson to her
home but never inside; we meet and associate with Lucy, the woman's
daughter, but Samson achieves a certain heroism for his "woman"
by never particularizing and naming her; she is always his "woman."

Lucy represents another peculiarity of Samson's: he likes young
nubile girls, aged 12-20. He is very much aware of their maturity
but is not sexually attracted to them nor they to him despite the fact
that he is in his early or mid-forties. The young ladies get annoyed
with him and his slovenliness but generally like him, though they
don't understand him. His feelings toward them is always fatherly
and "daughtery," or avuncular. Samson himself has a 12 year old
daughter by his earlier marriage, now going to school in Switzerland
but who comes to visit him in one of his books and he trains her
to be an assistant P.I., with the promise that she might become one
when she grows up. He is as far as I know the only P.I. who trains
his adolescent daughter to be a P.I.

With older women he is likewise not interested in sex; if they
try to get him in their domain generally he slides away with one
excuse or another. Twice at least, however, his joy with joking and
giving amusing figures of speech pushes him into perhaps ill-conceived
jokes. Lewin almost makes a fetish of bosoms. He is always noticing
the young girls' cleavage and once he says about a young lady secretary:
"The little secretary bounced out to meet me. She wasn't entirely little.
I caught a glimpse of two packets of Chiclets warming in her cleavage.
Hot Chiclets, forsooth!" (63) And in another book (*A Missing Woman*)
he has one of his characters (p. 26) refer to George Washington to
make a point when talking about a woman not being a virgin: "I
cannot tell a lie...but it's not exactly a cherry tree I cut down, is
it?" This kind of light-hearted flip humor results in a lot of interesting
and amusing one-liners.

In *The Enemy Within* (1974), he talks about a young man who
is working in a motel office and being very cagy about accepting
only high bribes for his information: "The body was young but the
mind was old" (8). Samson is working against a seedy Chicago detective
"who gives seedy detectives a bad name." "About himself Samson
says, "I'm more intelligent than I act" (31). But at another time he
admits: "I really am stupid sometimes. So stupid that even someone
as stupid as I am knows how stupid I am" (32). (Thus echoing the
Mark Twain and H. L. Mencken wit when they said they would not

join a club that would admit them as members.) Once he philosophizes: "Home is where the heart is. My home was burning. It came from TV dinners. Never mix two different brands" (65). Two other bits of wisdom come out in: "Day is day and night is night; sun in one, the next contrite." (128) and "Once stung twice shy" (*The Silent Salesman* p. 126).

His use of the one-liners often slips over into humor, sometimes enjoyable, sometimes a little strained, depending upon your own sense of humor. In *The Silent Salesman*, for example, he gives the rather local joke, "You haven't got any sense of Yuma" (176), and when the remark is greeted with a raised eyebrow of incomprehension, he apologizes, "Just an Arizonan quip." On another occasion (in *Missing Woman*) he tells the joke about "The guy marooned on a desert island with his dog. The guy eats everything in sight and then eyes the dog and, as he was chewing the last scrap of meat off it, thought to himself, Boy, Rover would really love these bones" (59). "I'd cooked my own goose, but I needed time to cook a few others and make a gaggle" (*Silent Salesman*, 202).

But though capable of some jokes of questionable seriousness, Lewin is very serious about his purposes and his novels. The plots are intricate.

In the first of the series, *Ask the Right Question* (1971), which introduces Albert Samson, the private investigator, Eloise Crystal, aged 16, hires Samson to locate her biological father. Samson has to do a lot of driving around central Indiana to work out the plot of biological and economic relations that tie together the daily activities and emotions of the two lines of the family in New York, Paris, and Indiana, the biological and adaptive, that tie together and separate the two lines of the family. *The Way We Die Now* (1971) is a story of blackmail and lewd pictures. The wife of a retarded man hires Samson when he kills a man while being used by one person to eliminate another. This is undoubtedly Lewin's most complicated and interesting story to date. In this book Samson is at his light-hearted though serious best. The tone is ironic but not heavy, not sarcastic. In *The Enemies Within* (1974), a woman leaves Kokomo because she is pregnant, marries another man to shield the child. The husband thinks his wife has killed their child, and mistreats her. So she runs away, goes to Indianapolis, lives chastely with her half brother as a man. The motive that triggers this unfortunate series of events was the woman's hatred of her profligate father who presumably fathered 6 illegitimate children around Kokomo. In *The Silent Salesman* (1979) Samson is hired by a man's sister to see why she can't visit him in the intensive care ward in the Indianapolis hospital. He and other medical men have been posing as FBI people and manufacturing and selling drugs. The brother is in fact dead but the other conspirators keep him on machines in a death coma so that they won't have to report his death and thus blow their cover. In *Missing Woman* (1981), the story is about a woman who wants Samson to investigate the disappearance of a former classmate from her home in Nashville, Indiana. But in fact the woman who hires Samson is not an academic from Connecticut interviewing for a job at IUPUI as she claims but is herself the woman from Nashville impersonating her friend who is supposedly hiring Samson to find her disappeared friend.

In developing his plots, Lewin visits numerous places in Indiana: Kokomo, Nashville, Lafayette, the IU Campus. He generally resists the temptation to make snide jokes about the various places. He confesses that he is prejudiced, as he says in *The Enemies Within* (p. 178), "Prejudice is a funny thing. Everybody has it; it's essential to balanced mental function." And he is prejudiced against the East Coast, as every Hoosier ought to be. In *The Silent Salesman*, Samson's mother warned him when he was going to the East Coast that he was "going the wrong way," and Samson later admitted that it was a mistake to go. In *Ask the Right Question*, when Samson has been put in jail and wants to relieve himself he asks if he can go "pee." The sergeant explodes in contempt: "Pee? Pee, no less. That's what a couple of years in the East does to people. They start peeing. Excuse *me* a minute. I got to piss." (166)

But Samson sometimes cannot pass up the opportunity to make a few snide remarks about Indiana localities. In driving to Kokomo, for example (*The Enemies Within*) he remarks, "The road had improved a lot since I first hitchhiked to Kokomo in the 1880s" (153). And in Kokomo he slurs: "Kokomo with nothing to do. Where had I heard that before?" He remarks at another point that Louisville, Kentucky is "not every detective's idea of a March vacation." (236) He has little respect for jails in general and Indianapolis' in particular. Thrown into that slammer he remarked, "It's not exactly the first time I'd been in the Indianapolis jail. But I hadn't been there recently. It hadn't changed a bit. They still needed to arrest a decorator." But he resists the temptation to blast Lafayette, Nashville, Indiana, and other places he visits.

Lewin concentrates on presenting Indiana pretty much as it is, given the need to reflect the light of his art through the needed prism. So he is not hard-boiled, smart alec, chauvinistic and mean. His streets are not as mean as those of the larger cities, he is not as flint-hearted as the chroniclers of those other mean streets. Perhaps his nearest accomplishment in the hard-boiled school is this passage from *The Way We Die Now*. On his way from Nashville, Indiana to Indianapolis, Samson has just picked up an attractive young female hippie hitch-hiker who turns out to be much harder than she had looked, and whom he likens to an asp. Samson comments on her attitude; and comparing her to his former wife:

My wife may have become a dragon when things didn't go well for me. But I'd rather be married to a dragon than a viper. At least with a dragon you always know where she is. With the clumping around and belching of fire.

I dropped the asp on Monument Circle.

In almost every way, then, Lewin's stories about the P.I. Albert Samson are interesting. Soft-spoken, self-denigrating, not caught up with self- seriousness or with developing a conventional American hero in the conventional hard-boiled way, he tells these stories of life in Indianapolis and the Midwest in a different and interesting way. His approach is humanistic, interested in people and culture more than in puzzles and games. This approach and development more than repay the reader interested in this kind of detective fiction.

The Ohio Valley of
Jonathan Valin

For simple, direct plotting and writing you can hardly beat
Jonathan Valin. Working in the American style (which may or may
not include the over-worked term "hard-boiled"), Valin writes directly
and simply of the world around him as he sees it, and his reaction
to it. His reaction is firm and unchanging. Though in him the world
is not peopled with heroes, it has its citizens of interest.

The world is best seen through his eyes. Limiting himself in
all but the latest work to the neighborhood of Cincinnati and Kentucky
just across the Ohio River, Valin depicts a world that is pretty much
distorted with evil holdovers of former beneficial institutions, with
evil in the heart of men and women, and with most people who are
out to help themselves only. But it has a few who are willing to
work for the betterment of society as they see it.

Harold Stoner, Valin's protagonist, in all his novels is no hero
living in a non-heroic world. He stands 6' 3" and is a powerful man,
but still he is a non-hero. "I'm no hero," he says in *Final Notice*
(p. 74). "I'm not in the savior business," in *Dead Letter*. (p. 18) Though
he later claims he is responsible only "for myself" (*Day of Wrath*,
p. 195), he isn't. He does not live the heroic life. He tends to look
backward rather than forward, to the former days of decency and love,
rather than to the chaotic days of today and probably tomorrow. He
loves the old-fashioned ways because those were the days when people
were likely to be more humane than they are today.

With a style that is enlivened by metaphor, one of Valin's most
permeating metaphors is that of the family, the real and the close,
the extended, and the community-world family. The trouble with
society is that the family has broken down.

The Lime Pit (1980) is a paradigm of most of the issues he will
take up in all his books. It begins with the loss of innocence because
of the breakup of a family, and one person's effort to act in *loco
parentis*. Old-man Hugo Cratz, too old to be sexually involved but
not too aged to need love and understanding, meets sixteen year old

Cindy Ann and asks her to live with him and take care of him. She agrees, and everything seems headed in a fruitful and harmonious direction. However, the idyll is interrupted with the disappearance of the girl, and Cratz suspects foul play. Though Cratz has no money, and Stoner is no hero, he decides to help out. Simply stated, Stoner says, "He needs me." Cratz's reasons for needing Cindy are likewise as simple:

> It ain't that you can find a young person that you can sit and talk to. They just don't care about the past. But Cindy Ann was different. And it wasn't like she was putting on. Boy, you get old enough and you can spot that sort of thing a mile away. She cared about me. Maybe having come from a broken home and being miles from it and folks and her friends she needed somebody to care for. (18)

No prude, Stoner is very much a moralist, and as he looks under the rocks of Cincinnati and surrounding society, what he sees works to turn his stomach. He sees too much. And what he sees as a Cincinnatian makes him sick. As he says, "You can't beat a real Cincinnati moralist for cheap, stomach-turning sentimentality. I like this city; it keeps me sane." (28) Later he says: "The moralist in me was getting a good work-out that day" (51).

Abuse of the weak by the strong offends his sense of human dignity. In this story, ignorant and immoral pornographers steal vulnerable young girls and get them on drugs, photograph them pornographically and sell them forever into lives of prostitution. Pornographers use children because they have a "grudge against the world," they are "trying to live out their childhood hurts on these children" (31). But the evil does not end in Cincinnati. The area of Kentucky just across the river (Covington, although he calls it Newport) is the sinkhole of the area. Newport's purpose in life is to:

> provide the gambling, the prostitution, and the sin that the good elders of our town have turned out of the city limits. Newport is an open secret, a dirty little joke that nobody laughs at because there's too much muscle and money in Newport to make it a fun or a funny place. It's a tough, leering border town, with a wide-open police department, a come-hither night life.

It's purpose is to serve as the sinning outlet for the sinning souls of people from Cincinnati and surrounding Ohio towns.

Throughout the book and later ones, the poignant sadness of life casts a pall over all happenings: "The poverty of some men's lives never fails to shake me," he says. In *Day of Wrath* he talks of a pastor who "spoke with the tired, shiftless, slightly servile voice of a man who had nothing left to lose. No pride, no property, no dreams. It was a voice that said, 'I just want to get by' " (p. 34). Anything he can do to re-enliven the sad music of human existence, particularly through the re-establishment of the family and morality in existence he will do—not just for money but for necessity.

The broken family and society serves as the backbone of the second book, *Final Notice* (1980). This book begins with a seemingly flimsier plot and possibility. Some sick soul is cutting the pictures of portions of nude women from books at one of Cincinnati's branch libraries. Concerned with the mutilation of the books, the librarians want the practice stopped. Stoner soon discovers that there is more to the mutilation than meets the librarians' eyes. Two kinds of deviants and sores on the body social confront Stoner in this book. One is kids. Though he has nothing against kids, he knows that they are necessary. Obviously, he is against new fads that bend them into all kinds of distortions, he is against what drugs and bad habits have done to today's kids. He is also against religious zealots and religious phoniness. Essentially, the trouble with kids is that they don't trust their elders, but then nobody trusts anybody else either. Perhaps with reason.

Stoner and his assistant librarian-detective chase evil-looking people throughout the city and countryside, looking for the obvious, only to discover at the end that it is one of the goody-goody looking persons who is the psychotic doing all the maiming and murdering.

The world is just as pretentious and phony, and openly attacking the family structure and the vulnerability of youth in *Dead Letter* (1981). A University of Cincinnati professor hires Stoner because his daughter, he says, has stolen some Top Secret documents from his safe. Again, the trouble is the family blown asunder by disease, greed and human failings. The truth is that the professor has been blackmailing people for seven years, hating his daughter all the time and intending to kill her. So he had been writing letters, signing her name, saying that she was going to kill herself. The plot is complicated because, as Valin's stories always reach out into the surrounding world, it gets mixed up in political radicalism, drugs, and blackmail. Again, moral love, family togetherness and morality could cauterize and stop the flow of blood.

In many ways *Day of Wrath* (1982) is perhaps more the true paradigm of Valin's work than the earlier pieces. It is more compressed, more direct, more compelling. Here, again, the themes are old. A school teacher calls upon Stoner to find her missing 14 year old daughter who is both almost too beautiful and too good to be true, according to picture and mother's account. Working with an uncooperative mother and society, Stoner traces Robbie Segal's path through the alleys and jungle of Cincinnati and adjacent areas until he discovers a den of prostitution, violence and evil that is almost unbelievable. Again, beauty and seeming innocence are not what they seem to be, and not what they used to be. But then neither was maturity and seeming decency. Here the self-indulgent wealthy were as much to blame as anybody else: One of the leading social butterflies of one of Cincinnati's most ancient and influential families was a "cultivated monster," and another rich, pretty girl was "like most talentless people, her only real gift was for self-indulgence" (p. 136).

And again Stoner's concern with the family gets him involved in the society of these monsters:

> It was odd, I thought, how easily I acquired families—how quickly I discovered relations in the most unlikely people. Or perhaps that was just another side effect of my bachelorhood or of my job. Perhaps those 'extended' families of mine were the only ones I'd every have. At least, that was the way it was beginning to look as I got closer and closer to forty.

Valin is strongest when he limits himself to the environs of Cincinnati and the surrounding Kentucky hills. There in a cocoon of his own building he knows the society, the people, their foibles, his own prejudices and loves inside and out. Especially he knows the people—his comments are always sharp, valid, telling. Once outside that cocoon he becomes less adept in his handling of the story and the people. In *Natural Causes* (1983), he moves out. The plot takes Stoner from Cincinnati to Hollywood, back and forth, working him not only in geography and people but also in a subject that people involved in one of TV's most popular soap-operas. The song is the same—sung to the same dismal tune: the evil that people do to themselves and to others. The extended family is perhaps even more extended, the people are perhaps even more revolting, both on the West Coast and on the banks of the Ohio River. But the intensity of feeling, of handling is adulterated by the geography. Some songs seem best played in constricted surroundings.

But from beginning to end, one characteristic of Valin's books is the neatness of the plotting. Though very much in the American hard-nosed school of detective fiction, Valin's books do not scatter violence for its own sake. Violence is there because people are violent.

Blood flows, as it must, but it is much less likely to be sprayed around all over everything than to be restricted to the places it would naturally hit. There are all kinds of natural body functions admitted, again, as occur in natural life. In Valin's works life is not prettied up; instead it might be made just as ugly as it can be. But these aspects are not gratuitous and unnecessary, not titillating. Neither is sex. Being forty and without family, Stoner is attracted to pretty women just as other detectives are. But he generally has only one at a time, and remains faithful to her.

Throughout, however, Valin's style is about as restricted, pure and effective as anyone's working in the genre today. He is not extravagant, given to high highs and low lows in style. Instead, there is a steady, unrelenting pull that draws the reader along without pain or hesitation, wanting to see what happens next. Further, although his language does not shimmer with the bright lights of Chandler's or Hammett's, it contains most apt metaphors that make it rise off the page. For example, he goes to his old Datsun that was "tucked like a nettle in a Bible between a Buick and an out-sized Cadillac." Money is "an orphan, a new limb waiting to be grafted on the family tree" (Pit, p. 8). One person was "one of those amiable old men who've become community property, like scruffy dogs. Everybody's meat" (Final Notice, p. 39). One Jesus freak has "a funny way of bouncing on the balls of his feet, as if he were getting set to go into the Big Game on God's Side (Final Notice, p. 85).

The combination of this style of writing, the subjects and environs he covers gives Valin an immediacy, a reality and an urgency that is compelling. No raiser of flags that flap in the winds of rapid-fire violence, Valin circumspectly asserts that the Ohio Valley in general and Cincinnati in particular are fascinating areas to write and read about.

The Triumph of Humanism in The Detective Fiction of George C. Chesbro

It has been previously pointed out in this book that the physically, mentally or emotionally exceptional person—the maimed, deformed, freaks, giants, dwarfs, the unusually beautiful and gifted, the the strangely ugly and the evil, the mentally disturbed— were often considered to have been somehow selected by the gods and therefore by virtue of their rareness were given special abilities or power. They were more nearly the children of the gods and therefore more nearly supernatural than the rest of us. These people differ from the so-called "normal" and are therefore cruelly isolated from the rest of us and have suffered long merely because they are different. They are different also from the detectives and criminals we have discussed in this book so far.

Classical literature, as Homer's works among others illustrate, was filled with unnatural creatures, half-god and half human but in every way superior. In Medieval and Renaissance times the hero, the wise man, was a Merlin creature or a hideous deformed dwarf who amused and advised such kings as Arthur and Lear. From the eighteenth century on the near-obsession with the freak and the exotic was carried on in Western Europe by people stocking zoos and museums with living and dead examples of the exotic American Indians, South Sea Islanders, Africans of all kinds. As they become more popular they were taken out of the zoos and put on the stages of freak shows, burlesques, minstrels and other kinds. So popular did they become, in fact, that showmen such P.T. Barnum exhibited them to the public in dozens of forms and all kinds of activities. He "Zulued" and "Tom-Thumbed" with every kind of act imaginable. This was one of the traditions that the authors of detective fiction who deal with the unusual and extraordinary draw on for validity and power.

The 19th century was also the Age of Darwin, and the introduction of the freaks and exotic people was on another level of search for the "missing link" in the chain of human development. As such they also represented the most savage, wildest, most natural of all creatures. Therefore they were the ultimate in naturalness, in unsophistication, of ugliness and deformation because they, like Caliban, are demonic. Their exterior ugliness is a sign of their interior sinful nature. They are therefore closely allied with horror stories, which are uncommonly popular today.

In detective fiction the hero, the protagonist, has always been a bit strange. Auguste Dupin, for example, was a recluse who wandered the streets only at night, keeping counsel only with himself; in at least one reincarnation of the Dupin-Poe character (Marc Olden's *Poe Must Die*, 1978) the "peculiar" aspect of the character-author is emphasized in a setting in which a giant English boxer is sent by Charles Dickens to America to protect Edgar Allan Poe from assassins who are determined to kill him. Julian Symons has the reincarnation of the spirt of Annabel Lee in *The Name of Annabel Lee* (1983).

Sherlock Holmes, the greatest of the Classical detectives, took pot shots at the apartment walls, shots of pot of a seven-percent solution, and played his violin while London shook. In the couple of dozen books that have recreated Holmes since Doyle killed him off, he is even more eccentric. In one (Fred Soberhagen's *The Holmes-Dracula File*, 1978) he is a confidant and worker with Dracula; in Loren D. Estleman's *Sherlock Holmes vs. Dracula* (1978) Holmes is called forth from the dead, as it were, to fight a rash of bizarre nocturnal crimes that is terrifying London. In Estleman's *Dr. Jekyll and Mr. Holmes* (1980) Holmes, at the Queen's request, was the first to discover that Henry Jekyll and Edward Hyde were the same person. In one book, Holmes is a born-again Christian who lives close to 221 B. Baker street and loves to play his stereo instead of a violin. To one biographer, Samuel Rosenberg, in *Naked is the Best Disguise: The Death and Resurrection of Sherlock Holmes* (1974), Holmes is literally the reincarnation of every kind of Freudian myth and hero from Jesus Christ on down to Satan. After Holmes, all detectives are unusual in one way or another.

The reasons for this abnormality are perhaps both obvious and abstruse. The role of the detective is to act as our surrogate superbeing, our statement of our own superiority, our effort to shake hands with the gods. As such the hero must be different from us, and this difference is marked by the physical, mental or personal qualities that the hero enjoys. But if the hero were perfect then he would be so superior to us in fact that he would make us uncomfortable; thus the role of the hero is at the same time to be superior and inferior. He must be imperfect, and therefore inferior. He is more easily distinguished as noticeably different if he has some physical or psychic abnormality, some eccentricity which sets him apart from us. And it is precisely the abnormality which seems to make him superior which in fact makes the hero inferior to us normal beings.

The detective hero may be tall or short, fat or thin; gregarious or withdrawn; hard-boiled or soft-boiled; violent or peace-loving; an insider or outsider; brilliant or apparently dull; loved by the police or wanted by them. In any event the detective's eccentricities paradigm his style, and his style communicates his individuality, opens him to our observations and therefore makes him vulnerable.

Normally an answering, individualistic ambassador of society— a protector of the community at large—the detective and his manner of work or play, and all those elements that comprise his very being and soul, remain one of the great appeals of any detective story. We wait for and applaud Father Brown's soft chuckle and quaint turn of phrase. We delight in Detective Lieutenant Columbo's crumpled overcoat. We scan the pages of a Holmes story for one of his eccentricities that transport our interests from one detective series to the next. Indeed, it is the fallibility of the infallible hero, the humanness of the superhuman champion, the weakness of our powerful surrogate that comforts our basic insecurity. That delicate balance between the *fantasy* of the superior and reality of the *inferior* must be struck in the storyteller's art if we are to be involved in his or her fictional world.

At times the eccentricities or outstanding physical or personal characteristics can be twisted into gimmicks, which perhaps more nearly caricature than follow the classical tradition. This was especially true in the pulps of the 30s and 40s, especially when in searching for a fiercely competitive market the writers had to outstrip their competitors in any way possible. The hero of Paul Ernest's novelette *Madam Murder—and the Corpse Brigade,* for example was Seekay, a private detective who had no face and wore a "cone" to cover his defect. John Kobler's detective, Peter Quest, had the unfortunate habit of losing his sight at the worst possible moments, and Nat Schachner's Nicholas Street was a victim of amnesia. Russell Gray's "Crab Detective" was forced to crawl along the floor because of his deformed body; and Gray's Ben Bryn possessed withered legs and tremendously strong arms. There were scores of others.

These extremes in detective fiction, like the numerous extremes one can think of from elite literature, are socially unfortunate and their use marks an insensitivity to the *feelings* of the member of our society considered in some way "defective." But the detective writer has a more immediate goal. In exploiting the misfortunes of others, these stories make those in society without the afflictions feel superior.

Today this kind of detective—at least in the shape of distinctly different individuals—has returned in rather strong force. The reasons for such return which were emphasized earlier in the discussion of Peter Styles include the speculation that the defective detective is a natural companion to the defective social and political society that we have created. Thus in such critical times, when the status quo is questionable, and the ostentation of the elite no longer fills the emptiness of our existence, we turn to myth, folklore, convention and formula (as witness the tremendous success of Romances and detective fiction today) despite or perhaps because of the condescending criticism of the elite and the continuingly widening gap between the elite and the "popular."

This basic threat to the fundamental essence of men is well revealed in the remark in *An Affair of Sorcerers*, the latest by George C. Chesbro (1979) dealing with the dwarf Mongo, when the dwarf's brother says to him: "I know you do all right with the ladies, although I have never understood what they find lovable about a smart-ass dwarf.... It's only logical that your first real love would be a witch." (p. 196)

This "freak" in today's fiction that I want to concentrate on is George C. Chesbro's Mongo, a 4 foot, 6 inch dwarf who is otherwise a Ph.D professor at an uptown New York City university. In developing this detective, Chesbro may have been influenced by the mentally retarded though he does not dwell on that aspect. But far more importantly he is calling on a different tradition that dates back at least to Homer. Dwarfs have always been world-wide in folklore and frequently have been thought to be remarkable wits and philosophers. Mongo the detective therefore is completely in line when he is the Renaissance person—a detective, university professor, former circus performer and black-belt karate expert; to a certain extent he is even a wit.

Chesbro's first book, *Shadow of a Broken Man* (1977) begins the theme that keeps him working in the most demanding and the most nearly "super" area of contemporary life, murder and international intrigue. Mongo's task is to find a dead man who really isn't dead. Working in the United Nations and against Russian intelligence and secret police, he ferrets out the guilty parties.

The second novel, *City of Whispering Stone* (1978), is somewhat more developed and more filled with intrigue. In this book, Mongo is called "a dwarf with a King Kong ego," and he needs this kind of self-assurance as he traces his quarry from New York, through the workings of the Shah of Iran's secret police, the SAVAK, to Teheran and finally to the old city of Persepolis. It is a heroic undertaking for a dwarf, and the artist of the art work on the cover caught the tone of the novel very well when he pictures Mongo standing beside a giant stone column in Persepolis. Symbolically, he is holding his pistol pointing straight out, and he is casting a giant shadow on the even taller column, there are four figures indicating this true heroic stature and its link with history: the gun, himself, his shadow, all cast against the magnitude of the Ancient Past. This configuration is emphasized at the end of the book, as Mongo and his regular-sized brother, Garth, are rounding up the villainess of the story, Neptune, a member of SAVAK. Mongo "imagined [he] could hear a soft wind filled with ancient voices blowing from it." And, as he says, he believes "in omens." They bury Neptune, the Agent they have had to kill, then Garth, the detective who actually shot her, sits near her grave for two hours. Indian style, with Mongo "hunched down in the sand 20 yards" away from him, waiting for ancient custom to end. Then they mount their camels and ride into "the blazing afternoon," looking back *only once* at the small mound they have left behind.

Of the three books, the third— *An Affair of Sorcerers* (1979)— is the most intricate, the most satisfactory, and surely the strongest example of Chesbro's effort to have his dwarf detective work in "heroic" enterprises and achieve heroic proportion.

This time he is called up to deal with an internationally-sponsored and financed group of Sorcerers, who are working with and through one of Mongo's colleagues at the New York City university. Mongo is called upon by the chancellor to investigate what is going on and to solve the mystery. He is led into the heart of the intrigue through a neighbor child (named Kathy) whose father has been working on a "book of shadows" which is the testament of the sorcerers he is working with. Mongo manages to infiltrate the covens of the sorcerers and to expose the ring leaders, who include another colleague from his university.

Mongo is captured, tortured, nearly killed, as is his brother, Garth, the regular-sized policeman on the NYCPD. But each helps the other to survive, and to triumph. That is obviously one of Chesbro's messages that people are strong when united, but there surely is more.

Chesbro uses the intellectual Renaissance man-dwarf succeeding in the regular world to demonstrate a point: that true love can be the agent to bring universal, or at least personal triumph. And he seems to have learned to reveal this in his third book.

Chesbro has been trying to say the same thing for three books but in the first two did not make his full statement. In *An Affair of Sorcerers* he has found his way.*Shadow of a Broken Man* ends with the four protagonists separated, two remaining together, the other two separated from each other and from the other two. But, as Chesbro says, "there would be an invisible but steel-strong thread binding us all together for the rest of our lives, a thread spun at one of life and death, trust and suspicion. I was intrigued. And I was afraid." Then the two people who are to remain together walk out together "into the smoky sunshine," one with his hand on the other's shoulder. This is a first effort at Chesbro's full message.

City of Whispering Stone moves Chesbro one step further toward his desired statement. This book ends when Garth has killed the villainess and saved himself and Mongo. Garth had felt he loved Neptune, Savak's chief female agent, as she was named, but Mongo had convinced his brother that Neptune was evil, and Garth had killed her in order to save his brother. The brothers say that they love each other. Garth asks: "Do you suppose this is what they mean by 'male bonding'?" And Mongo says he thinks so. As the two brothers ride away from the grave of the villainess Neptune, Garth, significantly, "looked back *only once* at the small mound we'd left behind" (my italics), Chesbro is halfway home in the statement he is trying to make.

In *An Affair of Sorcerers* Chesbro makes his statement much more comprehensively and effectively. One villainess has been discovered and destroyed. Another female—named April to symbolize Spring and the beginning of a new life for Mongo—has saved Mongo both physically and spiritually by giving of herself freely and willingly.

Having been in a sensory-deprivation tank for three and a half days, Mongo had been rescued by his brother Garth and taken to the hospital, and later to a hotel. Three days later he had tried to get up to go back to the hospital for his very necessary rabies shot. Describing himself, "a bag of skin has no desire, no fear, no will,"

Mongo had tried to isolate himself from all humanity especially April. He simply wanted to be alone, and not to talk. Realizing and stating his need to rejoin society, April ritualistically begins to cleanse him of his past and re-introduce him into the brotherhood of man. After she has begun and she has finished bathing him, she guides him to his bed. Then once he is in, she ritualistically begins to undress in order to join him. As Mongo sees the act:

> April struck me as the most beautiful and desirable woman I'd ever seen. Her skin was smooth and creamy, in striking contrast to the large earth-brown nipples on her full breasts. Bathed in the early-afternoon light, she glowed golden, like a Rembrandt painting.

As she slid into bed and "wrapped" Mongo in her arms, in his "exhausted state sex was the farthest thing from [his] mind. April was offering me her wholeness, her *self*. Lying in her arms, my face pressed against the soft flesh of her breasts, I could hear her heart beating; I felt safe." "Offering me her body was an *act* of love, not making love." It was the same selfless act which only women can offer that Rose of Sharon offered in Steinbeck's *Grapes of Wrath*, in offering to feed the man with the milk from her own breasts. From April's "self-sacrificing" encounter grew *natural* and loving sexual intercourse and a return to "natural" life: "The next time I awoke, April was no longer beside me. Perhaps she sensed in some way— *occult* was the only word I could think of—that I no longer needed her so desperately." He was safe and life had returned to normal.

April is Mother Earth in the spring, ritualistically joining herself with man—this time in its form of the superhuman dwarf and therefore man in a mystical manifestation—and a promising good on the issue.

Feminists, and some of the rest of us, might well say that this "sacrifice" on the part of April was the grossest kind of male chauvinism on the part of the author. But I would suggest otherwise. I would suggest that Chesbro is saying that self-sacrifice, that saving our fellowman and fellowwoman is the highest form of duty for the human being, and that though at times the going is tough because evil is powerful nevertheless the salvation can be achieved.

Garth, the everyday policeman and Mongo's brother, has brought reality into the lives of the people in the book. Mongo ends the book with the jointure of male and female bonding, as he closes the book and the message rather mysteriously: "I closed my eyes. Holding tight to both April and Garth, I let myself float away into the velvet darkness behind my eyes." I think the message is clear: There is a reality more important than the immediate and obvious, though that is important enough. That reality is *love*, and love which includes but is more than sex. It is brotherhood and sisterhood in the fullest sense of the words. Mongo as a quasi-religious individual serves as the bond between April and Garth, "holding tight to both."

Earlier in the book, Mongo has gone into a "cathedral-like" dwelling, and, with the lady of the house, has gone up to the second floor. From there he ascends to the attic on a ladder that can be lowered and raised. Once up he pulls the ladder up after himself and there all alone he searches among a thousand books for the mystical book of life. The parallel of this scene with that in Herman Melville's *Moby Dick*, when on a Sunday morning the minister comes into the Puritan church, climbs up into his pulpit and then pulls the ladder up behind him so that he can be alone while searching for his God and truth is so obvious that a reader assumes there are more similarities in the book. Mongo, like the minister and Ahab himself, isolates himself while searching for the meaning of life, and discovers that the meaning is love and brotherhood.

That seems to be Chesbro's fullest message to date, at least as he wants Mongo to express it. In his fourth book— *Turn Loose the Dragon* (1982)—he does not use his dwarf detective and he dives totally into international intrigue, which might be his way of waking up the time of universal love or, more likely, at the time of writing this book, he was more interested in developing his obvious love of international intrigue. Perhaps he felt that the earlier triad had completed his message.

Was Chesbro successful in his three books (and seven short stories) which involve Mongo the dwarf?

I'd say that his success is obvious. He has a hard, direct style of writing, which names and treats reality as most of us do, using slang and the vernacular when it is more expressive and more evasive circumlocutions might be used. Mongo has a fairly well developed sense of humor especially about the reality of his size. He never tries to dissemble, and frequently makes jokes at his own expense, as when someone suggests once that they keep a "low profile," and Mongo smartly answers that he always keeps "a low profile."

Most important, however, Chesbro always keeps perfectly clear in the mind of the reader that we are dealing here with ancient and venerable traditions which involve one of God's and nature's specially endowed types of people who can overcome unusual forms of evil. The books re-validate and strengthen that tradition, and in so doing remind us of one of the powerful beliefs of the past and perhaps one of particular merit for the future.

John Ball's Humanism

The motivating force behind the writing and thinking of John Ball is dignity and respect, the dignity of the human race, and respect for himself as a member of that race and respect through himself for all members of the race, American and foreign, black and white, pure blood and mixed-blood. Although he sees evil in what people have done in the past and continue to do now, especially social and racial intolerance, Ball believes that time—though it moves with glacial slowness—is an ally of compassion and understanding and will ultimately cause humanity to triumph over bestiality. In this respect he is probably more nearly like the Australian Arthur Upfield than any other author in this book. They have many characteristics in common.

Ball sees that people are different from one another, and different societies can seem to be threatening; yet all people are fundamentally the same because all belong to the human race. Ignorance fires most anti-racial behavior. Ignorance is the cause of the intolerance of the Southern white for the Negro, as ignorance and unfamiliarity is the cause of other whites hatred of non-whites. Ball seethes with disgust at what he sees as injustices. In *The Eyes of Buddha*, for example in Nepal, Detective Inspector Virgil Tibbs, who is a Negro, looks at the Nepalese around him "and although he knew little or nothing about the mountain people, he noted that they fell into different patterns—in features and in dress. He could not help wondering if he looked as strange and odd to them, a man with a skin far darker even than theirs. "Looking at them" he felt totally out of place; some of the fears of his early childhood in the Deep South surged back and he was once again filled with the feeling that because of his birth he would have to run somewhere far away and hide" (p. 137). Ball's most extreme statement of the feeling of prejudice of one race against another comes in his first, and perhaps strongest book, *In The Heat of the Night,* in which he has a Southern white (white trash) say about Negro boxers, but really about Negroes in general: "They don't feel it [pain] when they get hit the way you or I would.... They're like animals; you've got to hit 'em with a poleax to knock 'em down, that's all" (p. 5).

Although the sores of society have been festering for countless centuries Ball feels that time is an ally of compassion and understanding and will ultimately cause humanity to triumph over bestiality. As he says to the half Negro-half Japanese lady in *Five Pieces of Jade,* time is needed "in which society might come a little closer to evaluating people for what they are and not for their origins" (p. 72). But it may not take a long time. Certain customs cannot be changed overnight. For example, in *In The Heat of the Night* Tibbs solves a murder in a Southern town and in so doing saves a local red-neck's skin; although the man is grateful and even hints that he is appreciative things and customs must change at their own inexorable pace. As Ball says, the chief "thought of shaking hands with him, but decided not to. He had done it once and had made the point. To do it again now might be just the wrong action to take" (p. 152). The white man, Gillespie, hated the odor that he thought he associated with Negroes, and it would take a long time to have that myth dispelled. Also, poor whites in the South, according to Ball, have a near-insane hatred of Negroes, and it will take many lessons and much training before they feel that they can treat Negroes as equals without compromising whatever status they might have in the community. But the winds of change touch some people strongly. Within a few days of action in *In The Heat of The Night,* a red-neck who at the beginning of the book treats Tibbs stereotypically, agrees that there are some Negroes who are superior: "Virgil isn't a nigger. He's colored, he's black, and he's a Negro, but he isn't a nigger. I've known lots of white men who aren't as smart as he is" (p. 133).

Ball's hero is an Investigator with the Pasadena, California, Police Department. A Negro named Virgil Tibbs, he is a modified and modernized version of the classical hero type with the unusual and mysterious, or at least distant, past. His father had lived in the South close to the line of poverty and violence by whites against Negroes. Virgil had known first-hand prejudice and hatred and violence, and he lives in the books so close to his past that he is easily frightened by his place in society. In the first book, in fact, Tibbs is caught in a Southern town as he is returning from a trip to see his mother in a town even more rural, though unnamed, than the one he is caught in before. Tibbs is small of stature, about 5'9" and weighs 150-165 lbs, but he is very clever, an efficient investigator, and quite an actor. He is willing to assume virtually any part in order to root out the guilty in society, like Upfield's half-caste in Australia, Bony. In fact the similarities of Tibbs and Bony and the tensions of their two worlds are remarkable. He is in every way exceptional, as Ball says in every one of the books. For example, in *Five Pieces of Jade* the Chief of the Pasadena Police Department recognizes that Tibbs is exceptional:

Bob McGowan knew as well as anyone else that Virgil Tibbs had grown up under the near-poverty conditions in the Deep South, and for a Negro boy to rise from that beginning to become the man who stood before him now had taken much more than ordinary effort and determination" (p. 16).

Ball keeps up this attitude and action of the exceptional person throughout the books. Tibbs although very conscious of his background is indeed proud of his accomplishments, generally surprised because he has come so far since his father's time but reassured that in general he recognizes that his accomplishment, as well as that of society in general, despite horrible throwbacks to more aboriginal times, is real. Tibbs is proud of being an accomplished person, and perhaps more fiercely somewhat prouder than usual since he had farther to go than most whites. As Tibbs tells a woman of half-Negro-half-Japanese blood in *The Eyes of the Buddha*: "As far as I know my background is pure Negro; none of my female forbearers appears to have been raped by white slave owners" (p. 230). Yet at other times he is not ashamed of mixed bloods. As he tells the lady earlier: "Negro.... It's a word to be proud of. You have two heritages instead of just one." Then he comments on the esthetics of the union of these two races. "And...if anyone asks you, you are a very beautiful girl" (p. 185).

Her position, as well as Tibbs', is "profoundly difficult."

Time might be the only cure—time in which she might mellow somewhat but more importantly, time in which society might come a little closer to evaluating people for what they were and not for their origins" (p. 72).

Throughout Ball's works there surges a deep and profound humanism that makes him wish for the best in the human animal. He is against any kind of discrimination, in favor of good manners and genteelness, feels that the South has come a long way since Tibbs grew up there, insists that young people ought to be allowed to live their lives even if they incline away from the routes favored by their parents, and has a restrained sense of women's freedom. Mainly he wants an orderly, controlled world where people act decently to one another. It is a one-world-one-people attitude, one that accommodates and welcomes people of all stripes, one in which evolution moves along briskly but without militant revolution. "For centuries," Tibbs says sadly, "humanity has been living in little pockets all over the world; people kept to themselves because travel was difficult, or all but impossible." To the objections of the half-Negro-half-Japanese lady that she is a hybrid and therefore nothing, Tibbs makes a strong statement affirming the universality of people:

> A century ago—that's one hundred years—anyone like you would have been very strange, *but it isn't true anymore.* A century ago I couldn't have been what I am now; people would have thought me some kind of an animal that could be trained to do certain tricks, like shining shoes.
> "But at least you were one kind of animal!"
> Tibbs controlled himself and regained his self possession. "And so are you," he answered, "whether you know it or not. You're all human, all girl. I know you're a hybrid; so is all the best corn—they raise it that way." He turned her around until she had to look at him. "How many people alive today, do you think, are absolutely pure blood of one kind or another? Not that many. And they're not the lucky ones, because when you start mixing strains you get a better product most of the time. In horses, in plants, and in human beings too" (p. 104-5).

Tibbs, and Ball, are driving toward a classless society in which people are just people. In *Five Pieces of Jade*, for example, he is delighted when he enters an office and sees that his manner of behavior is genuine and so is a receptionist who "was no more concerned that he was a Negro than he was especially aware that she was an Oriental." Later in the book Tibbs reaches a point of jubilation when his chief of police answer Tibbs' query about the half-black-half-Japanese lady, "Do you know what she is?" with the answer "She's a human being." To which Tibbs responds, "God bless you."

Tibbs, having been cut off from the succor of society throughout his youth and still somewhat deprived of its full life-flow by prejudice around him in California, really is more vitally concerned with fraternity. He needs to mix and mingle with society, where companionship and love reside. All of Ball's books have this yearning as a kind of leitmotif. In *The Eyes of the Buddha*, for example, after a hard day's work Tibbs after dark goes to the Pasadena Hilton for a drink. But he needed more than liquor:

> He was not anxious for a drink, but he felt the need for contact with other human beings on a dispassionate basis. He wanted to be where people were, unconsciously still savoring the fact that he could walk into any place of public entertainment and receive the same courtesy and consideration as everyone else.

It had not been that way in his father's day. Most of the change in public attitude had come during his own lifetime, so that to him the new emancipation was still to some extent fringed with illusion: a roseate dream that could vanish into hard, hostile reality at any unexpected moment" (p. 25).

In *Cool Cottontail*, after a hard and trying murder investigation, Tibbs preaches understanding of nudist parks and practitioners and compassion for all. After the case has been settled, he heads for people and companionship: "he swung around a minor street excavation, straightened out the car once more, and headed down the famous street into the center of the city he called home." He is at home.

Johnny Get Your Gun (republished as *Death for a Playmate*), 1969, is perhaps Ball's most intense book, mainly because of the subject. A nine-year-old boy from Tennessee, living with his Tennessee family, is poor and badly fed and clothed. His family, living in Pasadena, is paranoid about their condition in life, their feelings of inferiority in Pasadena, and a natural belligerence that results. Ball is here concerned with two subjects. One is his near obsession with people from the South, perhaps strange when considered that Ball is from Minnesota. The other concern is Ball's heart-felt feeling about kids. Overall, however, is Ball's concern with law and order, with "civilization" as he would call it, and with law and order.

The nine-year-old, named Johnny, is condescended to by other school kids. One takes his only treasure in the world, a cheap radio with which he listens to the Angels play baseball, and breaks it. Humiliated, and following the belligerence of his father, Johnny gets his father's loaded gun and determines to shoot the boy who broke his radio. Frustrated in that effort he is wandering the streets when a carload of four black youths start to hassle him, and in the resulting fracus one is shot dead. Johnny, not knowing the youth has been killed but desperately lonely and afraid manages to get to Anaheim, to meet some of the Angels, to run from the police, but to be finally "tamed" by Gene Autry, owner of the Angels.

The book swings on the Constitutional question of the right to bear arms and Ball's contention that this Constitutional question must be interpreted for the good of society. Ball, writing through Virgil Tibbs' meditations, reviews the recent killings by madmen who "had the right to bear arms": John Kennedy, Martin Luther King, Robert Kennedy, other civil rights leaders.

The right to keep and bear arms was given when a raw young country was part of a great, wild, largely unknown continent. In crowded modern cities a loaded gun was as lethal as a pit viper."

The Constitution must be followed, Ball understands, (as when the villain in the story is captured and very carefully read his rights so that there can be no flaw in the trial that will follow) but civilization must speak to its holdings.

In many ways *Johnny Get Your Gun* speaks to the political turmoil of the sixties. Johnny is attacked by a carload of blacks. One has an older brother who is a black radical trying to foment riots in the streets of southern California cities. Stokeley Carmichael "had set the Negro's cause back a generation." The Rap Browns and others, according to Tibbs, are doing far more harm than good in the fight for dignity and rights.

This fight involves three groups. Johnny's southern family is fighting for dignity, work and happiness. The radical blacks are fighting for what they consider their place in the sun. Virgil Tibbs, himself a southern black and therefore encapsulating actually the feeling of both the other groups, is fighting for the rights of both.

As usual his heroic stature is clearly outlined. Ball carefully outlines Virgil's humiliated and unfortunate birth and growth in the South, which gave him a feeling of inferiority but determination to succeed. Ball carefully emphasizes how far Tibbs has progressed. Although he understands the prejudice he encounters even on the streets of Pasadena and LA, Tibbs is urbane and civilized. He is always considerate of others, whites or blacks, always carefully follows the law as modified by extreme sympathy, empathy and humanity. At times he finds the world is too much with him and he has to retire to his apartment, where he, in this book, consoles himself by listening to Ravel and reading the Book of Job.

Coming out as it did during the heat of the Civil Rights battles, the book suffered an interesting fate. As Ball tells the story, it went this way.

Shortly after Little Brown contracted to do this book, *Good Housekeeping* bought the condensation rights. However, someone there demanded that the black militant had to come out. Although he is an important character in the story, *Good Housekeeping* forced Little Brown to delete him from their hard cover edition. When Bantam reprinted the book, I saw to it that the original text was restored. Bantam wanted a new title, so I came up with one that read two different ways. It was my fifth suggestion and they bought it.

Though not his strongest artistic effort, somewhat contrived and too sentimental in its ending, for example, this book clearly was one of Ball's most powerful, at least in the effect, perhaps outside the circle of detective fiction readers, it achieved.

Four of his six novels involve the same detective inspector, Virgil Tibbs. The plots are strikingly different from one another both in locale and development. *In The Heat of The Night*, the first (1964), has Tibbs returning to the South to see his mother and to visit the places where he suffered as a Negro growing up in the midst of strong and muscular prejudice. On his way back to California, Tibbs happens to be in a small Southern town when a man is killed. Although the local law officials hate the thought they must for their own reasons ask Tibbs' help in solving the murder. After suffering from prejudice, he solves the crime and in so doing, by his exemplary behavior demonstrates that although prejudice is still rife it can be softened and mitigated.

The Cool Cottontail, 1966, switches, very interestingly, to a nudist park outside San Bernadino, California, where a non-nudist is murdered and thrown into a swimming pool in the park. This time Ball has two prejudices to work with, that against Negroes, as he insists on calling Blacks, and that against people who believe in nudism. Discovering that the murder is a play for power by the elite, Tibbs demonstrates again how proper behavior and time can diminish the evil of prejudice.

Five Pieces of Jade, (1972) switches to an exotic setting, that of a world-famous jade dealer living in Pasadena, California, a beautiful half- Negro-half-Japanese lady, the result of a union between an American soldier and a Japanese, and cocaine trafficking. Here Ball again has several prejudices working one against another and one against all. The trip through the book is a liberal education in the world of jade.

The Eyes of Buddha, (1976) begins in California but Tibbs' adventures take him to Nepal. The trouble in this novel is that a rich young lady rebels against the strict discipline of her father and runs away from home. This prejudice against youth making its own decisions is stirred into the ever-present one of Negro vs. White society.

All the books have a strong moral tone and a lean plot that makes the moral tone and a lean plot that makes them excellent reading.

John Ball is in every sense of the term a professional writer. That is, he writes for a living. But he is also a writer with the utmost integrity. He will not make a plot, write a detail or develop a point that has not been fully researched and authenticated. He checks his sources. But as an interested citizen he is very much concerned with American culture, and in his writing he analyzes and comments on this American culture continually. As a professional he turns to many kinds of plots and sets of characters.

Three have to do with a certain police sergeant, Jack Tallon, who had become disgusted with the life-style of the city and became Chief of Police in Whitewater, Washington, a small city of some 10,000 people. There he discovers that although the pressure is perhaps less, at least less diversified, he is confronted with essentially the same problems he would have faced had he remained in Pasadena. And Ball really has a knack for turning a new plot.

In *Police Chief*, (1977) Tallon has just been installed in Whitewater only to meet the same crime of rape that he would have met in Pasadena. This time, however, there is a new twist. The rapist wears a mask, but whether or not there is any real physical resemblance, the rumor gets around in town that the rapist is the new Chief of Police! Working under considerable disadvantage and duress, therefore, Tallon has to discover who the criminal is. Which he does.

But in this book, as in all of them, Ball lays his own philosophy and attitude toward society on the line. Unflinching in his individualism, steel-backed in his belief in the obligations as well as the right of all individuals, Ball is not one to be caught up by collective or assigned guilt, by those people who easily whine their way out of responsibility when caught. As he says to one of his associates at the end of the book:

> Frank, have you ever noticed that some of the most aggressive people become the most penitent when they get caught, or have to take the responsibilities for their actions? And they always have some kind of rationalization, some explanation that they feel gives them justification.

The second book in this series, *Trouble for Tallon* (1981), touches, again, on one of Ball's major interests for the past years, a religious cult led by an intriguing swami. A city councilman is killed and the citizens naturally suspect the Swami and his religious cult simply because they are outsiders and therefore different. Tallon plays along with the suspicions, even getting seriously suspicious himself. But he does what Ball suggests throughout his books as the proper course. That is, Tallon looks into all possibilities, accepts no accusations without proof, and gets to know the Swami. When he does he finds that the Swami is not only not the murderer but is actually positively on the side of law and order. The plot turns on several neat tricks, as well as thorough research and wide-ranging curiosity and knowledge.

Chief Tallon and The S.O.R., (1984) is another book developing Ball's interest in the strange, the esoteric and the fraudulent. This time the plot turns on the annual convention of a group called the S.O.R., the Society for Open Relationships, a group of radical sexual practitioners. Presumably leading their own lives in their own way, without harming any other members of society, this group asks only that they be left alone. But a television evangelist named (naturally) Ezekial Moses finds out about the group and sends in his fire and brimstone to try to force them into eradication. Tallon, believing firmly in the First Amendment to the Constitution, is not precipitous in accusing, relying instead on tedious and thorough research to bring out the truth. Again, he does.

These books represents what is perhaps most interesting and most realistic about the police procedural. Before writing the books Ball researches his background thoroughly. As he says in the "Author's Note" to *Police Chief*: "This work was made possible because of the extraordinary help and cooperation of Chief Jerome Gardner of the Cheney, Washington, Police Department. He, and everyone in his organization, supported this project from its inception and made many significant contributions." These books are data and facts backed by lively and fascinating story-telling.

These books are also enlivened by a kind of firmness and strength that is gratifying. Obviously, Ball likes to tell the stories, and looks forward to the next. This might seem strange in view of the fact that the books are always advertised by John Ball, "author of *In The Heat of The Night*." Ball's strongest books are, in fact, those having to do with the black detective working in Pasadena, California. With him we get to know and love the black detective through his adventures. So far, at least, there has not been enough exposure to make Tallon the loved police chief that Tibbs is. But Ball may be planning additional studies. Anyway, he leaves each of these books with an eagerness, a spring to his step that promises more. There is simply more in the conclusion of each of these books than the hook to get you to buy and read the successor. For example, at the end of *Police Chief*, the first in the series, with one job just finished, Tallon knows that there will be others, and that he can handle them. As he says at the conclusion:

But whatever it was, he would handle it. He would have to, because that was his job and his responsibility. He was the top man on the totem pole. Whitewater was depending on him, and he knew that he would not let his city down."

That is, in fact, the philosophy of John Ball in this series and in all his other books. If the world is not counting on him, he at least has a contribution to make, and he will make it—unrelenting, uncompromisingly, stiff-backed and somewhat formal, but with genuine compassion.

Ralph McInerny:
Religious Detective Fiction
in Chicago

Chicago is the site for the works of at least 150 detective fiction authors and probably 1000 novels. Some are excellent—like the works of Thomas B. Dewey—some are less successful, but all tend to be thoroughly American with one degree or another of hard-boiledness.

In this Chicago setting there are several authors working in the rapidly developing school of religious detective fiction, or detective fiction about clerics written for a larger than religious audience, an audience necessary if the authors want a wide readership. In fact it seems that Chicago and Detroit (and possibly Los Angeles) might well be the leading cities in this particular sub-genre. In Detroit there is William Kienzle, whose works, because he is an ex-cleric, tend to be heavily larded with doctrinal and Catholic messages, not to mention a lot of miracles, though Kienzle is such a gentle and humorous, and excellent storyteller, that his works are interesting. He wants to write stories, mainly about Catholics but for non-Catholics as well, which keep the reader guessing about the outcome until the author himself reveals the secret. His works are English in derivation and development.

Chicago itself has at least three people writing today using the immediate environs and religion as location and subject matter: Andrew Greeley and Charles Merrill Smith, and Ralph McInerny. Greeley is much better known for his more general novels about the Catholic church and his concern with God as a woman, his use of storytelling as a method of getting God's message over to the public. He has published some criticism on detective fiction in TAD, has published a short story or two and has just brought out his first full detective novel, *Happy are the Meek*, which involves a cleric named Father Blackie Ryan as detective-priest, totally given over to the closed-house style armchair detection of Nero Wolfe. *Happy are the Meek*, incidentally, charts a new course for detective fiction and surely one

that will be followed by others: at the end of the novel there is appended
an additional chapter called "The Prologue to Andrew M. Greeley's
next Blackie Ryan Mystery *Happy are the Clean of Heart.*" That
approach out-hangs all the cliff-hangers of former fiction.

Amongst the Protestants the most prolific religious writer of the
Chicago area is Charles Merrill Smith, whose detective hero is ex-
pro-football quarterback with the Los Angeles Rams, C.P. "Con"
Randollph, minister of the prestigious Church of the Good Shepherd
in downtown Chicago.

In many ways Randollph is the Perfect Protestant Prelate. He's
tall and handsome, possesses a body that makes female Protestants
pant, has a grace and cool style that comes from his experience with
football players, the media and the very rich. Randollph is everything
that the Bible teaches some people to be: he ministers in a church
that is in downtown Chicago and is attended only by the wealthy
and powerful, with a token poor person or two. Randollph is not
waiting for death to usher him into the Heavenly pleasures. He has
them here—an admiring housekeeper to tend his every want in his
penthouse pastorate, only the finest food, wines and conversation with
the most beautiful people. When he marries he weds the lovely and
vivacious TV personality Samantha Stack, who has a life and will
of her own. Their life together is doubly beautiful, doubly cool and
doubly conspicuous in the fast lane.

Perhaps the careful and attentive reader with the proper
perspicacity needed to sniff out the high comedy and irony needed
to appreciate the detection capers of someone who more than has
his cake and eats it too will appreciate this fiction. But to many readers
it will seem that Smith is taking detective fiction out of the mean
streets of Chicago and placing it on the golden avenues of an earthly
paradise. A far more engaging, human and worthwhile series of
detective fiction is that written about Father Roger Dowling and his
sidekick Captain Keegan, of the local police force, by Ralph McInerny,
a professor of Medieval Studies at Notre Dame University. Actually
McInerny has two series, the one about Father Dowling, and another
about a nun named Mother Mary Theresa, written under the name
Monica Quill, and plans another which, he says, will be less concerned
with religion and religious topics.

The ten books in the Dowling-Keegan series are placed in St.
Hilary's rectory in a small town 40 miles west of Chicago named
Fox River. Father Dowling, some fifty years old, is an ex-legal specialist
in canonical law about divorce and an ex-drunk who was allowed

to rusticate in an out-of-the-way diocese where his distaste with canon law and church practice and other maladjustments could be worked out or hidden.

Dowling is assisted in his police work by an old classmate, Capt. Keegan, a policeman who once studied to be a priest, but instead took up the law. The whole business looks like it might be stickily religious. But such is not the case. The leading characters are very human and the world they work in is real. There are, also, various secondary characters, the most notable being Dowling's housekeeper Marie Murkin, who live and breathe the air of naturalness. McInerny gives the reader all the Catholic local color that is needed, but not nearly enough to be overwhelming as Kienzle's books are. Further, there is a healthy and very human tension built up between the man of the cloth and the man of the uniform over the role of law and order in society. In *Her Death of Cold* (p. 50), McInerny states explicitly Keegan's hard-nosed legal and social creed: "Anyone is capable of anything. And everyone must pay for what he has done. That was elementary. That was justice. Without justice, life would be a mockery." But Roger Dowling represents the diametrically opposed point of view. Deeply aware of "the foibles, the weaknesses of the human heart" he began to stoop in his posture in a manner suggesting that "he was willing to shoulder whatever tragedy was brought to him." As a result of his vision, Roger Dowling's eyes "moldered with mercy and he took on a lidded look to conceal at least partially his vulnerability to others' pain." But Dowling is no starry eyed dreamer. As McInerny says in John Reilly's *Crime and Mystery Writers*, Second Edition, Dowling "may seem soft on sin but he is hard on crime" (p. 635).

Throughout the series there is a gentle humanness and sense of humor on the part of Dowling, which often go hand in hand, who despite trying to remain aloof from the weaknesses of the flesh, since he had early experienced them, sinks again and again into the slough of compassion. Although he realizes it may be vanity, not to mention somewhat absurd, he cannot avoid likening his fate to Dante's, whom he admires and whom he thinks he resembles in trying to ease the hard road of the human race to Paradise.

But the most satisfying aspect of McInerny's books is the empathy and humanity—the humanism—which informs them. The books are written about and by an understanding soul who has learned a lot from the teachings of the Bible.

The first of the series, *Her Death of Cold,* sets the style and tone of all the others to follow. It is a story about an old unloved woman, preyed upon by fortune-hunters and resented by her children. Father Dowling is called upon by the woman to comfort her in her fear and last days, and along with Captain Keegan to solve her murder when she passes on. Dowling's character is clearly outlined: he had always been deeply "affected" by the cases he reviewed as a canonical legal expert in marriage and divorce. "He felt at one with the other humans whose weakness had brought them low" (p. 35). McInerny shows the priest's heart bleeding for the poor souls whose lives had been tied together in marriage and doomed by the Church to eternal worldly misery. This anguish had driven him to drink; this Church prohibition actually drove William Kienzle out of the church because he could not practice it. But though Dowling was a priest first and a detective second, he did have a nose and a curiosity for snooping which made him eager and delighted to hit the trail and to stick with it until the guilty had been apprehended.

The book ends, the mystery solved, with a gentle tension between Dowling and Keegan over their opposing philosophies of crime and punishment. The officer insists that "Society cannot be maintained if things like that go unpunished." The priest insists that "Society is built on unpunished crimes."

The Seventh Station, McInerny's second novel, is more complicated than the first. It has to do with Dowling gone on a religious retreat to get away from the world and back to his soul; the title comes from the various stations the priest worship at on their retreat. But things don't work out for Dowling to have solitude and meditation. A mad priest takes murder into his own hand, a private investigator takes blackmail into his, and Dowling and Capt. Keegan must unravel the mystery. Although McInerny's humanitarianism has settled down somewhat at least in overt statements, he and Keegan agree that the plea of insanity in capital cases and the lawyer's abuse of the plea cause great damage in the world. Nevertheless there are people who are not sane enough to be held accountable. At times the setting and characters in this story are so intense that the situations must be leavened with more humor than was evident in the first book. Even here, however, it is restrained. For example, in speaking about Blaise, the ex-priest who committed the murders, McInerny says:

But the fact is that Blaise had tripped. The inauthentic Franciscan had in his haste caught his foot in the skirts of his robe. Blaise would have been wise to have remained defrocked (p. 211).

Lying There (1979) is a rather conventional detective story. This time a man wants to get into the munitions business and hires as his bodyguard an ex-con who turns into a murderer. Again Dowling turns out to be an effective detective because, as he says, he "just can't help speculating about the police's quarry." But Dowling's motives are quite different from those of his friend, Capt. Keegan, and of the police in general. Dowling's are here, as in all his other books, for love and humanitarianism: "A human being is the object of an infinite forgiving love."

In many ways *Bishop as Pawn*, (1978) is McInerny's most successful novel if success means his overriding message of the brotherhood and needed love of man. In this story McInerny is most explicit in his statements that Dowling is aware of the fallen nature of man, our meanness and pettiness. But he knows that we all want and need love and that God's love, though hard to find needs to be sought. The plot is about several unhappy and broken marriages and the kidnapping of a bishop for ransom.

But McInerny's most explicit statements in this book about his continued thesis about love comes not with Dowling as his spokesman but with a renegade priest named Chirichi who has been defrocked but who continues to look upon himself as a priest and to perform the rites of Catholicism working from a kind of Churchmobile, under the authorship of God. Undoubtedly he represents McInerny's concept of what the ideal priest would be if he could, because Chirichi sees only God as his bishop and pope, and he follows God's teachings not the Church's. "People were meant to come together, not be divorced by theories and rites and theology." he tells Dowling. He continues to chide Dowling:

Doesn't it bother you that love gets all wrapped up in rules and laws? That's bad enough for just ordinary things, but its a scandal to think we can control the flow of God's love.

In a remorse that touches his own failings and those of the Church he represents, Dowling admits that "The broken souls [Chirichi] dealt with were the mainstream" (p. 40). Although the world is not ready for Chirichi's kind of church, the book ends with Dowling's more practical, though humanitarian, philosophy: Contrary to Keegan's feelings that eyes must be paid for eyes, teeth for teeth, life for death, Dowling knows that "Mercy would have its opportunity" (p. 231) in the system of justice.

Sometimes McInerny's stories are less effective than they generally are. In *Second Vespers* (1981) he seems to have an unconventional and fuzzy detective novel. The characters are not well outlined and sketched in. The plot is rather unbelievable because the characters don't act sensibly. The plot turns on the various sexual peccadillos going on in a small town and the blackmailability of the citizens of the place. A famous author is living on his estate with his sister after having the world told that he is dead. One of his sons by an earlier wife comes to town seeking to find his father's estate in order to destroy manuscripts because he thinks his father's reputation needs to be protected although he hates his father anyway. The book is less detective story than *Peyton Place* with an Oedipus overtone, with Father Dowling and Capt. Keegan acting out their roles as detectives only in the second half. Again, however, McInerny's humanitarianism shows through in explicit statements.

In this novel, as in its predecessors, frequently this humanitarianism is aired in a recounting of Dowling's trouble with the canonical law of the Church and his reaction to it; from that Dowling's feelings flare out into broader scope:

> The guilty party is each of us. No man is without sin. No court, no code of law, can undo the past, make what we have done as if it have never been. We are what we have done. A new self can be created only by a prolonged sequence of deeds. Not by a ruling, not by a judgment that events which occurred never really happened.
>
> Yet it was impossible not to share the mad hopes of the majority of those who came before the court (asking for divorce or annulment of marriages). There was not a chance in the world that their marriages would be annulled, but the flaring hope for a new beginning, the unfounded belief that, in a different setting, untrammeled by past promises, one would be a completely altered person, capable of nobility even heroism, was contagious. Understanding that dream, knowing it was doomed, not wanting to thwart hope precipitously yet fearful of raising false expectations, Roger Dowling led a life of participated anguish (p. 39).

In evaluating McInerny's fiction critics have likened Dowling to Rabbi Small and Father Brown. In fact he is not similar to either, and the comparison is too easy and virtually meaningless. The characters in McInerny's fiction are perhaps less well-rounded—less full—than Kemelman's. They may lack the bemused gentleness and fuzzy-headedness of Father Brown. But on a larger scale, McInerny's characters are surely more successful than those of Leonard Holton, his stories more successful than those of the California writer. They are more successful, at least to this reader, than Kienzle's. In other words McInerny's characters are realistic, lifelike, believable and convincing.

On a broader and more interesting intellectual scale arises the interesting question of why so many clerics (and academics) are writing about themselves and their vocations these days, two areas which in the past were generally excluded from the genre of detective fiction. In other words why are there so many detective novels now set in religious settings and college campuses and written about academics and clerics? One explanation is of course that these are the areas that the authors know, and since academics and clerics are turning to writing they must use the materials they are familiar with. Another reason is that a growing number of readers are interested in the goings-on in academe. Two areas in our world which in the past were somewhat sacrosanct are being democratized into mainstream life.

To open up public exposure in religion is a move that has been going on since the beginning of Christianity, especially from the 14th century in the works of John Wycliff, William Tyndale, Martin Luther and other "heretics." It has always been resisted by conservative church people, as it is today. Education also has been reluctant to raze the wall that has surrounded the monastery-like region of higher education. But generally it is being demonstrated that forcing religion and education to go public makes them more accessible to the people, therefore of greater concern to people and ultimately all of society is the gainer. The works of detective fiction in this effort, in Chicago and elsewhere, is very useful.

Martha G. Webb:
"Somebody's Sweet Little Aunt"

A writer of remarkable police procedurals is Martha G. Webb, who also publishes under the names Lee Martin and Anne Wingate. Although under her three names, Webb writes different kinds of novels, as one would suspect, there are several aspects in subject matter and attitude which permeate and energize all the works. One is the theme of violence and her particular concern with it. Her law-breakers are young people, young men and women, boys and girls, who have not started out on the right path in life and who therefore suffer. Hers is a world of young whores who try, sometimes successfully, to manipulate men but who are in turn generally mistreated by the men; drug pushers and addicts who indulge in all kinds of violence to sell and obtain their drugs; motorcycle gangs who terrorize the community; people who are victimized by crime. But throughout the main theme of Webb's novels is compassion and empathy for the vulnerable, the misfits, those who have never been able to work their ways into and in society. She believes that they can find their ways in society and life, can reach self-respect and dignity, and in so doing contribute something to the human race. Webb's main concern is compassion for the human race. Each book betrays a heart beating with a general concern for humanity.

Webb is a former policewoman who has first-hand knowledge of the subjects she writes about. At first she was a policewoman in Atlanta, Georgia, then in a small town in Texas. She places her fiction in small towns, in Georgia and Texas. Because she writes of the small towns of the South and Southwest, she has a different ring about her stories than those centered in the maddening crowds of cities. There are fewer people in her stories, but the crimes and violence are essentially the same as their larger counterparts. Her stories ring with the authentic sadness of universality and of timeliness.

The work of a police department in even the smallest town goes on unabated, hour after hour, day after day, year after year. The policeman in next year's black and white sedan, wearing a wash-and-wear synthetic uniform shirt, carrying a stainless steel .38 is the lineal (and sometimes direct) descendant of the last century's town marshal with his sugarloaf head and heavy .45. The crimes change only slightly; husbands and wives still fight each other, drunks still shoot up bars, and if yesterday's horse thief is today's auto thief the intent is still the same.

And rules for fighting crime, and the humane treatment of the inhumanity of crime, remain virtually unchanged.

Trying to solve the crimes and understand the criminals, Webb is caught up in a layperson's concern with the psychology of criminals. To her they seem always warped by society, even as society is warped and pitted by them. As she says in *Too Sane a Murder*, she is not a psychiatrist, does not "know anything about how these things work, schizophrenia, psychosis," and she broods over whether a person could "have flipped out" and been a murderer. And she wonders if a mentally deficient person is morally guilty of crime when he doesn't know what he is doing. The courts generally say not legally guilty, but society often says morally guilty nevertheless.

In an early book, written under the name of Anne Wingate, Webb begins her treatment using a young punk-like man and another man who is old enough to be the young person's father. Young Thomas John Inman is a castaway on the ocean of society. "He'd never found a job he wanted to do, a man he respected, or a dream worth following." And that is his trouble—as well as society's. Smoky Liam O'Donnell, the older man, is the town's only detective and main operator in cases of drugs and kinky murders. In this small town of Overlook, Georgia, 13 people in all are murdered, 6 young girls, many of them obvious sacrifices. The guilty person, somewhat obviously, is a university professor who for his own reasons has to get rid of persons after he has used them. Inman, in an effort to find himself, infiltrates a motorcycle gang that is peddling drugs, gets beaten up several times, but in the end finds himself, establishes a splendid relationship with Smoky, who turns out to be far more than a mere police superior, and gets set to live as a useful citizen. He had found what he needed: "...a job, and a dream, and somebody he could respect—and also that elusive quality he'd never known he lacked called self-respect". This accomplishment exemplifies Webb's major concern: with the proper attitude from society, many people can find the self-respect, love and dignity they need. This theme develops more and more as Webb works through her later books.

It is the theme, with a somewhat different emphasis, in *Darling Corey's Dead*. The theme is again alienated and vulnerable people in a cold and somewhat indifferent society. A lady police officer has suffered an unhappy marriage and divorce. From that she has come away cold, frigid and afraid. She can operate as a police officer effectively, but she does not want to cross the bridge into human relations as far as she is concerned. Another main character is a postal inspector who has suffered the same fate and pretty much wound up as cold, indifferent and vulnerable. But they are not the only persons thrown into the world vulnerable and wounded. Darling Corey is a young black girl who is beautiful, mean, indifferent, and quite competent of manipulating men. But she in turn is manipulated by The Man—who, though he masquerades on the decent side of society, is cold and indifferent to suffering. Nobody "shoves [him] around anymore." There are others who are brutalized by society and forced into becoming everything other than decent law-abiding and loving people. But the evil results from alienation and misapplied power. In the end, the breaks in society are papered over, at least, because the vulnerable mature out of their frightened state into strength, and since they are strong it was all right for them to love because nobody could catch them unawares and wound them.

Her first book, *Too Sane a Murder* (1984) written under the name Lee Martin concerns a giant of a twenty-six-year old man who obviously is retarded in brains but is well ahead of time in heart. Accused of killing four people, this man, named Olead, is pretty much indifferent to the world around him because he does not believe that anybody cares whether he is railroaded into guilt or exonerated.

But Webb's compassion and concern, voiced through the female police officer, is clear. Her soft-heart becomes clear to everyone almost immediately. A fellow-police officer says that she looks "like somebody's sweet little aunt." Her husband tells her that he has often known "her head" to go wrong but he has never "known [her] heart to guess wrong." And she confesses to one and all that when she knows someone is wrongly accused of a crime, she goes all out to clear him.

But it takes more than a warm heart to make an enjoyable novel about the way the police work and the people they work on. This novel is such a book. The characters are alive, the situations are realistic, and Webb's style of writing is steady, clear and fascinating, with a touch of Georgia-Texas that gives it a character all its own. Though she feels vulnerable in the world, her own family, at home, is "cocooned in a comfortable mess of newspapers, magazines, popcorn, and the televised football game." In having the opportunity to play with a child, she feels "a baby short, in playing time."

This is a complex and complicated novel, which Webb works out with consummate skill and readability.

The same kind of theme and attitude permeates her other novel, also. *A White Male Running* is a somewhat different approach to the police procedural. This one covers a somewhat different and much more complex segment of society. A wealthy and successful black lawyer has decided to run for political office. But there is a shadow over his past. As a twelve-year-old he attacked a white man who was murdering a woman. He made a serious cut on the man's throat and thought he had murdered him. Then instead of running to the police, the Texas of his youth dictated instead that he hide the attack and hope it would never be discovered. But it is, and he is being harassed and threatened by the white man whose throat he cut and supposedly murdered. The plot of the book is, however, not that simple. A junior officer of the police department is working underground among cocaine bike riders who would just as soon murder as sniff. In addition the book is permeated with the evil that a psychopathic murderer in the tradition of Jack the Ripper is perpetrating, killing women, especially those who are pregnant and seek abortions, every chance he gets.

But the various strands of the plot are interwoven nicely and clearly, making the story rich in human weakness and acts and crimes.

Mainly, though, Webb's world is mitigated by the compassion of the police officers. Though it is more hidden in this book it is nevertheless present.

And Webb's style of writing maintains the clarity and directness of the earlier book. Again, it is vernacular and home-spun. As for example, one person's description of a woman's breadth across the hips: "I mean she five ax handles and a plug of chewing tobacco across the rump."

Her writing is effective. Her thinking is clear, her sympathies very warm and human. Her world so far is impressive. One can only assume that it will continue to be enriched in the future.

Webb's latest novel, *Even Cops' Daughters*, written under the name Anne Wingate, carries on the several themes she has worked on through her preceding novels, but this time with a different emphasis.

Her scene is Farmer's Mound, Texas, again, and her male protagonists, though she has several protagonists in this work, are Tommy and Smoky, the young man who serves on the police force as an undercover agent especially in drug cases, and his older superior, still a major portion of the detective section of the police force. This time Tommy infiltrates the Dragon Biker gang because they are running drugs, and the police need the information they can supply.

But this time, Webb's obsession with the wrong done young and vulnerable people, especially girls, is more intense. Jackie is the eleven-year-old daughter of a black police officer and a drunken whore. Jackie is assaulted by a white man. Webb had first written that Jackie had been raped, but her editor at Walker publishers wanted the attack changed to assault, apparently thinking that rape was too violent; Webb gladly changed the charge. The black, beautiful child assaulted by a white man is a significant development in Webb's subject. This time her concern is with integration of blacks and whites in a police force, and the liberation and dignity of women. So black and white men police together, and black and white women police together, that is by the end of the story. It takes a while.

There are several women who are assistant cops that are full-fledged bona fide police. They are not necessarily sex symbols; on the contrary, Webb seems to be drawing them realistically. She therefore says of one that she is not pretty but is "a woman who could think." And think she does, and in fact all the women do. They fulfill their duties completely. In the end, two female officers, one black and one white, arrest a wanted criminal, marching into the police station proudly, and almost to the applause of the whole force.

In many ways, this is Webb's most complicated but least complex novel. The themes of abused youth, of misdirected youth, of alienation and abusive power are present, but more important matters seem to be the perhaps larger issue of women's and men's dignity working together, of women's liberation, and of integration. Working out these themes satisfactorily is not a small accomplishment. They are the same issues, as we have noted, that obsessed most of the writers we have seen in this volume. They are the issues which concern most American writers of detective fiction.

Webb accomplished her goals in direct, vernacular, natural-non-artificial writing that breathes with authenticity. She does not alter or mute any language because she is a woman. She calls a rape a rape, a vomit a vomit, a bleeding wound a bleeding wound. Her language is authentically Southern, with numerous southern expressions not used elsewhere in the country.

With her skill in language, her concern for the social and humanitarian issues, Martha G. Webb— "somebody's sweet little aunt," as she half-facetiously refers to herself—is more than a little old lady writing for the mere fun of it. She may well develop into a major voice in police procedurals with the whole of the American scene—and all of humanity—as her field of concern. She is well along the way now.

Christie Tea and Chandler Beer Martha Grimes' Early Detective Fiction*

Among the scores of contemporary British and American detective fiction authors who continue the tradition of the Golden Age in writing about British subjects in British settings, there is one new writer who mixes her love for the tradition with a healthy touch of the "mean street" philosophy of Raymond Chandler; in other words she mixes her Agatha Christie tea with warm suds in the pubs. The writer is Martha Grimes, author of three books so far, *The Man with a Load of Mischief* (1981) and *The Old Fox Deceived* (1983) and *The Anodyne Necklace* (1983). In many ways they are typical of the modified classical school but, for some of us at least, fortunately they are also strikingly different despite the fact that some readers and reviewers are classifying Grimes as Christie's literary descendant. Grimes, incidentally, insists they are wrong.

They are surely typical in the affection shown for the British scene as the proper setting for detective fiction. Grimes, a professor of English at Montgomery College, Takoma Park, Maryland, has traveled widely and observingly throughout the British Isles, all eyes and sensitive pores, soaking up every bit that she saw and heard. As professor of English literature, she is addicted to literary allusions and quotations. Her combination of local color and customs, history, literature and folklore and culture enriches her books deeply. She is also keenly interested in the theatre and her first two books incorporate plays and celebration as vehicles on which to swing and develop the plot, so that in effect, like Shakespeare, whom she obviously deeply loves, she has plays within novels or drama within drama to develop her art.

Like Christie before her, Grimes believes that one murder is likely to beget others, so she is not economical in her crimes. *The Man with a Load of Mischief* for instance, which takes place in a small town in Northamptonshire, has four, and all are unusual if not

After the works studied in this essay, Martha Grimes has continued to turn out at least one book a year, sticking to the locale, cast of characters and essential development evidenced in these earlier books.

*Reprinted permission of *The Armchair Detective*, 129 W. 56th St., New York, NY 10019.

grotesque. The first is a man garrotted and his head stuffed into a keg of beer. The second is discovered hanging, covered with snow, on the signpost of the inn, up so high that not the first person observes the absurd figure swinging in the wind. Another murder is committed on stage before the eyes of the audience in a presentation of *Othello*, and one near-murder is just avoided by the detective dangling over a steep and tall cliff, literally hanging by his fingernails.

Grimes is more economical in the number of murders in subsequent novels but the jarring abruptness of the crime is hardly diminished. In the third book, for instance, a young girl is fiddling in a London Underground station for pennies when she is apparently purposelessly smashed over the head; the plot is complicated that ties this attack in with a murder in the village of Littlebrone, 40 miles away.

The first novel turns on the greed of a former player who pits one female love against another and covers his tracks so carefully that only a clever detective could uncover the truth. Grimes reveals the guilt of the person in a variation of the closed-room solution that is amusingly satisfactory. The following two books are somewhat more open in their solutions.

All three books are complicated. The first is as rich and intricate as an old elaborate footrug. The second develops on a possible double of an heiress who left home eight years earlier and who might well be prevented from returning so that various people might profit by inheritance, marriage or some other means. After a second murder, the detective finds the murderer just in time to prevent other violence. The second novel develops on a city-wide reenactment of *Twelfth Night*, when people are in disguise and when therefore murder and escape might be easy, and is surely fraught with great possibilities that the wrong persons might be killed. The third novel develops around the murder of a young woman and the mutilation of her hand on the fingers of which are rings in a village 40 miles from London, the somewhat unnecessary murder of another woman who happens to be in the wrong place at the wrong time, both murders being connected to the theft of a piece of jewelry named the Anodyne Necklace and drug-related activities.

In all three books, the settings for these manifestations of man's humanity to man, or generally to women and teenagers, are a country mile from the conventional British mystery. Out of a realization that there are too many detective writers jostling one another in the castles and country estates of Britain to make detection work there profitable and enjoyable, Grimes has placed the actions of all three in or near country inns and taverns. Her eyes describe and caress the old inns as though they were the haunts of all the worthwhile people of the past. They are also excellent places for crime. At one point, Grimes has her detective ask if there could possibly be a single inn in all of Northamptonshire that has not had a murder committed in it.

Grimes has worked out rather successfully the at-times ridiculous and artificial situation of the detective (official or private) and his helpers, and the tension that arises between and among them. Her leading detective is Inspector Richard Jury, a man stationed in London who goes out to the provinces when he has to but reluctantly and with considerable grumbling. Like the books in general, which Grimes develops as a kind of paean to Britain, Grimes thinks of Jury as *the true Englishman*—and to Jury, as Grimes says that is "the ultimate compliment."

His helper is Sergeant Wiggins, a bumbling dope who can just manage to follow directions. He always has the sniffles and requires medicine. This affliction and requirement Grimes turns very neatly to Jury's advantage, for at least once it saves his life. This pair is assisted and frustrated by Chief Inspector Racer, also from London, who tries to supervise and help Jury. They always have an unofficial helper in the person of Melrose Plant, who is around in all three books, a woman named Lady Agatha Ardry and various others. Although Inspector Racer is arrogant and proud of his record, Jury and Wiggins are humble and don't mind at all having other people assist them or solve a murder. In general, Jury and Grimes think people take things too seriously. Throughout the books, there is a light-handed approach to the reality of life, though she has two or three aspects which are obviously of great concern and importance, and usually she confronts them with a directness in approach and language similar to that of the successful British detection novel writer Ruth Rendell, for one.

One serious aspect is Grimes' concern for and interest in people. They are the same kind who frequented Hogarth's and Dickens' works at an earlier period and are seen today in such writers as Michael Innes (especially. See *The Daffodil Affair*) or Julian Symons' works without the duplicity and meanness found in his characters. Grimes has a special fondness for children and dogs and cats. Most are preternaturally bright. She weaves them in at times in less than obvious but always enjoyable and helpful ways. They are a strange group of human non-humans. In *The Man with a Load of Mischief*, for example, she has a set of waifs, a boy and a girl about twelve-years-old, who appear, almost by accident, and become an integral part of the plot. When confronted by Inspector Jury and asked their names, the boy replies that his name is James but the girl is so shy (or devilish) that she will not answer the questions. So Jury names them both James, the boy is James I, the girl is James II. She is happy to be so named. The two kids help Jury track the person who committed one murder and provide him with a slingshot, a gift that is going to save his life later on. In *The Old Fox* there is another curious boy aged 12, named Bertie. In *the Anodyne Necklace* Grimes has several groups of her shadowy kids, but her main one is Emily Louise; she is more realistic than her predecessors but unfortunately not as effective. Grimes states in correspondence that she has "a rather obsessive interest in kids" and that what she does with them "is no doubt owing to something in [her] own psyche." As readers we hope Grimes will continue to tap the deep well of that psyche. Perhaps equally amusing is the gifted dog Arnold, in the second book, that plays the old folk game "Simon Says" and saves Jury's life. Grimes is not sentimental about kids and dogs—she is instead surrealistic. These "animals" are the essence of life.

They are symbols, perhaps, of the waywardness, the vagaries, of human nature. They are wild and untutored, yet sensible and useful in a mad world. They at least of all people actually make sense, though at times Grimes seems not to have yet learned exactly what they mean to her and how she is going to handle them. This uncertainty, in fact, is their strength. As soon as she begins to make them more normal, as in *The Anodyne Necklace*, they become less interesting.

Certain aspects of nature, likewise, virtually monopolize her but she might not quite know what to do with them. The most obvious and most compelling is snow. Snow is as important in the first two books as is air to breathe. The first book begins in a quiet snow fall, snow hides the body of the second victim hanging on the sign outside the inn. Snow provided the virgin territory which is dirtied by the footsteps of the murderers and desecration of snow provides castings of the steps which Inspector Jury uses to pursue the murderer. The second book, *The Old Fox Deceived*, ends with a kind of prayer to snow. As Jury winds up his investigation of the murder, he steps out into the weather, and Grimes turns her prose to snow; "The snow wasn't sticking; he wished it were. He wished, as he walked down the High, that there were great heaps of it—dry, white untrammeled." Grimes' greatest paean to snow, making it a worker of magic and transformer into the Great Mysterious, occurs at one of the high points of the ending of *The Man with a Load of Mischief*. When Inspector Jury wants Vivian Remington, one of the lovely women in the book, and his favorite, to love him and she refuses and walks away, she comprises one of the powerful symbols of the whole book: she is "making another neat line of tracks across the unbroken snow," and as she enters a house, "from this distance it was like watching a doll go into a dollhouse and shut the door behind her." She recedes into the distance and into a different form and existence.

As is frequently the case in these books, Grimes has powerful symbols working though they don't always point explicitly and sharply at her meaning.

Her symbols and messages—in fact most of the burden of at least the first book—coalesce in one set of symbols. In *The Man with a Load of Mischief* as the plot works and Inspector Jury is cornering the murderer, the scene begins to unfold in the local church. Jury is in the pulpit discovering a diary that he knows has been left there, an important book in revealing the truth, and the murderer enters and stands below Jury in the pews, with his gun ready to shoot. He knows that Jury has no gun, thus symbolically no power. The murderer begins to taunt Jury and to shoot at him. Jury snaps out the light, moves around to avoid being shot, and then saves himself by employing two very mundane artifacts given him earlier: One is the slingshot given him by the two children James I and James II. Jury uses as his rocks for this slingshot some cough drops that the ever-ill Wiggins dropped in his pocket earlier. With these simple worldly instruments, Jury shoots out the colored religious windows of the church. Each shot makes a loud bang as it burst the holy windows, thus creating a diversion which allows Jury to escape until assistance comes. Readers who are symbol sniffers can do a great deal with this scene. It well exemplifies Grimes' style of thinking and developing—the mundane with the spiritual, but more of the former than the latter.

In many ways the delight of the books is Grimes' style. Her figures of speech are homey, yet closely observant, and many of her best are from the world of children and animals, especially animals. For example she has a gray cat bestir itself, his "face besotted with sleep." In another instance she describes the same animal, a "gray brindled cat slipped from the sill and walked toward the back...pregnant with ownership." I would like to see Professor Grimes' own household.

But perhaps Grimes' most effective, most fondled and caressed, writing is used to describe those country inns that she seems almost obsessed with. A few lines from *The Man with a Load of Mischief*, used at the very introduction demonstrated her whole attitude.

The English inn stands permanently planted at the confluence of the roads of history, memory and romance. Who has not, in his imagination, leaned from its timbered galleries over the cobbled courtyard to watch the coaches pull in, the horses' breath fogging the air as they stamp on dark winter evening? Who has not read of these long, squat buildings with mullioned windows, sunken, uneven floors; massive beams and walls hung round with copper; kitchens where joints once turned on spits, and hams hung from ceilings. There by the fireplace the travelers of lesser quality might sit on wood stools or settles with cups of ale. There the bustling landlady sent the chambermaids scurrying like mice to their duties. Battalions of chambermaids with laundered sheets, scullions, footmen, drawers, stage-coachman, and that Jack-of-all-trades called Boots waited to assisted the traveler to and from the heavy oaken doors. Often he could not be sure whether the floor would be covered with hay, or what bodies might have to be stepped over or crept past on his way to breakfast, if he slept in an inner room. But the breakfast more than made up for the discomfort of the night, with kidney pies and pigeon pies, hot mutton pasties, tankards of ale and muffins and tea, poached eggs and thick rashers of bacon.

Grimes likes to play around the way with such old inns were named. Her folklore and etiology are extensive and accurate. For example she talks about the way the "Bull and Mouth" inn got its name: It was named in commemoration of the taking of Boulogne Harbor by Henry the Eighth, and the "Bull and Mouth" sign was a loose rendering of the Boulogne Mouth. She assumes that another inn, the "Elephant and Castle," does not derive from the many folktales told about finding elephant bones in the vicinity or an escapade of Eleanore of Aguitaine but from the howdow on the elephant's back. Grimes suggests that the origin of the name for the inn "Goat and Compass" was the prayer "God Encompasseth Us." And "The Iron Devil" came from the French word "Iirondelle." To all of us, because it was also an American tavern, perhaps the most interesting derivation was for the inn "Bag o' Nails," which came quite logically from a misunderstanding and mis-spelling of the word *Bachanals*. Grimes loves these bits of English lore.

The question arises as to the place of these books in contemporary British detective fiction and their impact on the trend. Of course it is premature to evaluate their effect at this point, but there are certain features which seem obvious. So far the effect has been steady and growing. Grimes is getting a steadily increasing readership. There may be only a small "school of Jury" but this school is ever-expanding because Grimes' hero does have a strong and starkly outlined personality and Wiggins, his assistant, is both credible and delightful, more so than many other side-kicks, for example Leo Bruce's Sergeant Beef. Her other characters are richly developed even those who make cameo appearances—like the children on whom she lavishes vivid though brief attention. But humble detectives like hers, no matter how thoroughly developed, develop national and international reputations slowly; hers will come.

Her books are realistic and there are few writers working the same vein at the moment with greater strength, Michael Innes and Julian Symons, for example. Grimes' is a peculiar and unique strength. Her most powerful aspects are the settings—those old and musty and secretive and delightful ancient bits of architecture, the country inns. She knows and loves the countryside and the inns—and paints them surrealistically. In *The Anodyne Necklace* she is less concerned with the inn than with a necklace also called by that name. This book is, therefore, in setting and inn-lore less interesting than its predecessors; many readers will believe that Grimes' earlier particular and peculiar approach to the country inn life of Britain constitutes a vein of literary gold that she could have made her very own and through it enriched our appreciation of the British side of the genre had she had not decided to broaden out into more conventional areas.

She is in this treatment developing her setting in quite a different way from others, of Leo Bruce, for instance (1903-1980) in his Sergeant Beef and Carolus Deane series, which work essentially the same territory. In both Bruce uses the same geography—small villages, country lanes and woods—and the country tavern setting. But with a major difference, especially with regard to the taverns and pubs. Bruce likes the territory. "There's always a pub in your cases," says a character in *Jack on the Gallows Tree* (1960; 1983). "I believe you like all the phony darts-with-the-locals stuff." Bruce does like the atmosphere so he can use it to milk the locals of their information. Sometimes his inns are places to be hated. In *Furious Old Women* (1960; 1983), for instance, Bruce has a tavern overrun by religious zealots who display on a table a sign that says "There's an Inn-Sign on the Road to Hell." To Grimes, on the contrary, an inn is far more than a mere building or setting. It is an organic character pulsating with history and life, often more important and alive than many of the characters.

Be that as it may. Throughout her books Grimes' attitude toward everyone is bemused understanding. She does not cattily condescend to some of her people, a la Agatha Christie; they are all worthy of respect in their own right. In the wide range from the humblest to the most aristocratically pretentious Grimes finds them all amusing; oftentimes her most loving attention is poured on the lowly and ignorant, whom Grimes obviously feels most comfortable with and on whom she lavishes her most detailed development.

Grimes' books are powerful comedies of no-manners, of the assumed gap between the blue-blooded and red-blooded people and how both types flow through the same channels in rural England. Her people are delineated in Hogarthian outlines, vitalized by Dickensian gusto but characterized by a detached humor and understanding that make them distinctly and exclusively Grimesian; her people just don't look and act like other Britishers. They and their world are fascinating, far more enjoyable than the conventional British detective fiction world. At this point she really has no superior in what she does. Her world is enriched by every new novel she turns out, and our admiration grows.

In a greeting and toast to this fine new writer, readers of British detective fiction will want to raise their pints of appreciation to Grimes and sing out "Long live the country inns, the peculiar animals, Richard Jury and his group of assistants and those marvelous surreal children." Long write Martha Grimes!

Sherlock Holmes as Christian Detective: The Case of the Invisible Thief

In our society with its decided political and religious swing to the right there has been, curiously, a tilt (or rather a rush) also back to Sherlock Holmes, despite the fact that on the surface at least, Holmes, although obviously a political and cultural conservative was hardly a practitioner of Fundamental born again-Christianity. The two movements may be merely coincidental, but in at least one instance there is a direct connection.

In the swing back to Holmes there have been numerous reissues of all his works in new paperback editions. And there have been numerous (over three dozen) resuscitators and imitators. There have been, for example, such books as *Sherlock Holmes in New York*, based on the NBC adventure written by Alvin Sapinsley, adapted by D.R. Bensen (1976). *Murder by Decree* (1979) is an adaptation by Robert Werenka from the screenplay by John Hopkins; it centers on Jack the Ripper. A series of murders is projected into the future in *An East Wind Coming* (1979), by Arthur Byron Cover. In this fantasy the murderer is the wolfman, in a society peopled by newspaper people and godlike men and women.

Realizing that there can be only so many hitherto lost manuscripts about the adventures of *Sherlock* Holmes, lucky authors have come across the hitherto unpublished accounts of *Mycroft* Holmes, Sherlock's shadowy and intellectually superior brother. *Enter the Lion* (1979), by Michael P. Hodel and Sean M. Wright recounts an episode of Mycroft getting himself involved in a plot to overthrow the American government and reestablish British control through the Confederacy. In *The Adventures of Sherlock Holmes' Smarter Brother* (1975), by Gilbert Pearlman, based on a screenplay by Gene Wilder, a new brother, named Sigerson Holmes, is involved in what is in comparison with the original sedate adventures a wild and burlesque tale of sex and ridiculous adventures.

The appeal of Holmes and his world has proved most popular. There are perhaps a dozen volumes of detective works by Doyle's contemporaries, for example three volumes edited by Hugh Green— *The Rivals of Sherlock Holmes* (1970), *More Rivals of Sherlock Holmes* (1971) and *The Further Rivals of Sherlock Holmes* (1973)— *The Rivals of Sherlock Holmes* (1978) edited by Alan K. Russell, *A Treasury of Victorian Detective Stories*, edited by Everett F. Bleiler (1979) and *Beyond Baker Street*, edited by Michael Harrison (1976). These and various others contain stories by Victorians who complemented if they did not rival Holmes and the detective story of the time.

Another interesting thrust in this general tradition of resuscitating Holmes is Michael Dibdin's *The Last Sherlock Holmes Story* (1978), one of numerous stories based upon the sensational and terrifying near-obsession of writers with a particular kind of violence and fear and hatred of women as seen in a reexamination of the Jack the Ripper story. In Dibdin's story the information for the study is drawn exclusively from *The Complete Jack the Ripper*, by W.H. Allen, 1975. Holmes, under the influence of Prof. Moriarty is shown to be Jack the Ripper, and dies falling from the Swiss mountain cliff into the Reichenbach chasm, in the same way he had fallen in Doyle's original story.

Perhaps the most remarkable treatment of the new Doyle-Holmes factory is the dazzling study of the Holmes canon and person by Samuel Rosenberg (1974), *Naked is the Best Disguise: The Death and Resurrection of Sherlock Holmes*, which follows in the tradition of the earlier study, *The Private Life of Sherlock Holmes*, by Vincent Starrett (1933, 1960, 1975). Rosenberg, who has filled among many positions that of monitoring for the movies all outright, apparent and even faintly insinuated acts of plagiarism, demonstrates in his famous book that Sherlock Holmes was, among other persons, collectively and individually, Friedrich Nietzsche, Oscar Wilde, Dionysus, John Bunyan, Robert Browning, Boccaccio, Napoleon, Frankenstein and his Monster, Gustave Flaubert, George Sand, Plato and Socrates, Anthony and Cleopatra, Henry Ward Beecher and Sodom and Gomorrah. As Tennyson had Ulysses boast that he was a part of all that he had met, so Doyle, according to Rosenberg, was a part of all that he had read—or rather all that he had ever read was a part of him and evidenced itself in the thousand faces of his hero Sherlock Holmes.

A less flamboyant but entirely interesting book of fiction is the imitation Holmes story, *The Case of The Invisible Thief*, one of a series of Baker Street Mysteries by Thomas Brace Haughey (Bethany Fellowship Inc., Minneapolis, 1978). This is one of the few if not the only detective fiction series written by a confessed born-again Christian whose open and avowed purpose is to demonstrate the need for Christianity and power of prayer and at times does so in the most unexpected and dangerous places and times.

Haughey is, or was, the English Program Director of missionary radio station KVMV-FM in McAllen, Texas. According to the information in the front of his book, he holds a Th.M. from Capital Bible Seminary, a diploma from Rio Grande Bible Institute Language School, and has done evangelism and youth work in Mexico and has taught in a Bible School. He has also edited a Jesus Paper and done considerable writing.

Despite his zeal Haughey feels somewhat nervous and defensive about using detective fiction as an instrument for evangelizing. In the preface to the *The Case of The Invisible Thief* he self-consciously defends the medium by pointing out that there is nothing wrong with escapism. Such great Americans as Abraham Lincoln and FDR used mysteries during war time, delighting in seeing a villain "get his comeuppance." Undoubtedly Lincoln and Roosevelt were not unaware of the similarity with their wartime goals, for as Haughey points out further in the Preface, ever since Medieval times, morality plays have demonstrated that virtue pays. Sin destroys. That same theme lies at the heart of virtually every detective story worthy of the name. Crime is followed by doing time. The good get the goods on the hoods.... Deep down [the readers] know that situational ethics is baloney. And they welcome the simplicity of clear-cut right and wrong."

Not all readers like the stories for this clear-cut change, of course, and Haughey admits that not all detectives have been "pillars of virtue." But each fought "against an evil greater than his own." And undoubtedly Haughey, whose favorite detectives are Perry Mason and Miss Marple feels that his fight against irreligion is a greater battle than against mere mortal evil. Haughey's detective, Geoffrey Weston, is "the only detective old enough to vote who—as Jimmy Carter would put it—has been born again. Weston battles evil with a passion."

Mason may be Haughey's favorite detective, but obviously his model is Sherlock Holmes. Haughey's parallel is close. The book begins with Geoffrey Weston, the detective, and his Watson (the narrator, named significantly John Taylor) having breakfast in their bachelor apartment at 31 Baker Street, a site chosen because Weston "took delight in recreating the rustic air that so characterized his grandfather Mycroft's celebrated brother," and selecting this Baker Street address which "Gave us a mystique that had attracted clients," for this enterprise of "Sleuths, Ltd., London's Consulting Detective Firm" "God had been good" to them. Weston has all of Holmes' prescience and air of playing tricks. For example, at the very beginning of the book when Taylor unconsciously glances at the ledger, Weston surprises him with a whole paragraph about how one should work for pleasure and not worry about money. And in another bit of Holmesian stagecraft, Weston announces before the man arrives and knocks on the door that there is a stranger coming who needs their help.

The setting for the mystery of the story is about as closed as it could possibly be. From the Pinehurst Laboratory in England, which was absolutely security safe, some valuable papers have been taken directly from a safe in an office which has keys held only by reliable persons and is under 24 hour surveillance of cameras and guards. A real question is how somebody could have gotten in without the camera eye having seen him. That problem, however, is soon solved by a demonstration that since TV cameras have no depth perception it is relatively easy to provide a fake wall of the same color as the real wall behind which one can walk. Furthermore, the safe was opened while an invention was used in the camera to create the illusion that the machine was not there. The author's explanation was that "The invention used in the robbery created the same illusion from *every* angle. The thief was encapsulated, as it were. Memory circuits froze the picture while the safe was being opened."

Of far greater importance in the story is the question of what kind of secret work was going on in the laboratory. It eventually becomes clear that the work was ungodly and conducted by people who do not believe in Christian principles, in God himself, or even in Spirit. Therefore it is easy to believe that the secret work being conducted at the laboratory is genetic engineering, as eventually comes out.

Working from the assumption that cloning is the most ungodly of activities because it denies God, strips people of spirit and humanness, Haughey repeatedly hammers away at his concept of what constitutes a good Christian and the needs of a Christian society.

Weston discusses the existence of God and the needs of a Christian society with a learned scientist who is a moralistic materialist. Weston insists that "law only works with people who consider it to be grounded in an absolute—sometimes not even then. Without citizens that have convictions concerning right and wrong society would crumble." Weston insists that the scientist's "definition of law makes law (if you will allow the use of the term) evil."

Not believing in God is bad enough. Not performing Christian rituals is evil. But apparently not living a Christian life is even worse. One of the scientists in the book is a Hindu, for example, and that mere fact alone makes him suspect as a murderer. When the Hindu starts lamenting that there is no love, no good on earth and, under hypnosis, tries to commit suicide because of his desperation and loneliness, Weston grabs his gun and tries to wake him. He reassures the despondent man by telling him "There's god. There's truth"— that is, of course, Christian truth. And Weston punctuates his reassurances with slaps on the man's face, apparently believing that at times any heathen deserves a little bit of muscular Christianity.

Although experiments cloning are still being carried on at the laboratory, and there are large fish tanks containing little foetuses and operating as their "mother," according to Weston, apparently there are clones already abroad in the city, or evil forces that conspire with the clones, because Weston penetrates a Satanic cult meeting of clones one night and saves himself only by invoking the name of Jesus Christ, just as John Taylor one night on a stakeout had saved himself from the crushing weight of evil only by invoking the name of Jesus Christ. Perhaps author Thomas Haughey is closer to the truth than we recognize. For Sam Rosenberg in his book postulates that Doyle had "Holmes equate himself with Jesus."

As the plot winds down, the robbery at the Laboratory is revealed to have been done by the young "man" named Peter Heath, who was not a human being but a clone. He did it, he killed his foster father, Arthur Heath, to prevent him from revealing his unnatural parentage and the kind of experiments taking place at the laboratory. Peter, although immune to most reasoning and pressure, has to reveal his identity and the truth about his act when, as in witchcraft exercises through the ages, he is commanded in the name of God: "IN THE NAME OF JESUS CHRIST, I COMMAND YOU TO ANSWER. WHO ARE YOU?" Weston commands. With a cackling giggle and saliva drooling from between bared teeth, the clone with "A halting, rasping, hollow hiss breathed an ancient message: 'I AM LEGION, FOR WE ARE...MANY'.''

This twist on cloning had been tried a year earlier in the book *Exit Sherlock Holmes*, by Robert Lee Hall, with even a more bizarre twist, where genetic engineering had made Holmes and Moriarty apparently part of the same genre, and as Holmes says "more than brothers." In that book the union is destructive.

But in *The Case of the Invisible Thief* the evil done by the cloning and by the materialistic belief that there is no such thing as spirit and soul is checkmated by Weston. He convinces the scientists that their ungodly materialism is destructive. Even the official on the police force, Inspector Twiggs, confesses that he would like to hear more about Jesus Christ, and John Taylor, the narrator, smilingly says that he has all night to talk about that subject.

Now if you think that this book sounds like an insufferable sermon about a bigoted and stupid detective who interrupts his detecting at crucial and dangerous moments to pray then you are not quite correct.

Haughey does interrupt the flow of the story to deliver philosophical-religious debates and homilies. For example, he once sermonizes:

> You remind me of a man who once asked 'What is truth?' If you really want to see what a soul is, look at the souled. Then look at the soulless. Subtract the second from the first. What you have left is the essence of humanity.''

His tilt is openly four-square and born-again Christianity. His points are made in uppercase emphasis.

But there is a general geniality and lightheartedness about this Holmes-Watson pair which in some ways is as pleasant as the originals. These latter-day Holmes-Watsons have very jolly times in their bachelor quarters in the vicinity of their models. They enjoy their Holmes-Watson breakfasts and general actions. Weston eats Spanish peanuts instead of shooting cocaine, and listens to stereo records instead of playing the violin as Holmes always did. In general Haughey does not take himself too seriously. He is delighted with his punning, which can go on to embarrassing lengths, on the name of the Inspector, Twiggs. For example: "Ah, Twigg! You're just the sapling we've been looking for. We'd as leaf have Twigg as any tree in the forest." There is little violence, and it is conducted offstage where possible and there is none of the heavy handed prose of such right wing writers as Mickey Spillane. All in all the book is an amusing and pleasant experience.

It may be difficult, therefore, to see why the author was not successful with this detective pair. Apparently he wrote two other books, but they are not readily available.

If, as Sam Rosenberg had insisted, Doyle had created Holmes at least in one of his many guises as Jesus Christ, the parallel is too subdued and covered to be effective in the present world. Maybe the detective mode is not the right vehicle to teach Christianity and love per se. Perhaps readers would like to say that the swing in America to the right is not as far and as complete as we have been told. Perhaps not. However, the truth apparently is that despite the obvious and far-reaching resuscitation and continued vitality of Holmes in nearly every other area of present day American life, the right wing, regardless of its size, is not reading detective fiction. Perhaps these people are not interested in stories of Jesus Christ as detective. Perhaps that is the only present-day area in which the ubiquitous Holmes does not work well.

The Border
Through Canadian Detective Field
Glasses

Borders—and the tensions, clashes as well as the peaceful opportunities created by them—are different things to different people. To some—the more conservative and those who need the comfort of restrictions—they are comforting and reassuring. Borders provide edges of existence, the beginning and ending of things, the starting and stopping, life and death, the alpha and omega. Yet with their restrictions borders provide complete freedom, something as in literary terms the regular 14-line sonnet form provides the freedom to address and cover any subject.

To others, however—those who do not need the physical or psychical restrictions, the ability to see from the beginning to the ending, those who do not like to look upon things in a linear fashion—borders are restraints and restrictions. They cramp one's style. Rather than providing opportunities for movement beyond a known point, borders tend to inhibit, slow down and bring to a halt.

But to all people borders set patterns. They tend to summarize the past and to control and predict the future. They serve as chokepoints through which life's patterns, habits, attitudes, culture flow, and the borders control those movements. The tensions set up that these rites and passages create are often debilitating or worse.

Borders exist in virtually every area of life, both physical and mental. There are borders of religion, ethnicity, sex, family, culture, linguistics, psychology, morality and politics, to name just a few. Some are so "natural" or seem to be that they go almost unnoticed. But some, like the political ones, become at times very obvious and chaffing. Political borders can be "natural" or artificial. Those based on natural divisions like rivers, mountains, oceans, even those based on historical events of great magnitude like battles, seem to make more sense than those which are merely arbitrarily located and imposed.

Borders are for everyday life. As long as life runs in the accustomed patterns, they fit and can be useful. They can join as well as separate; they connect as well as disconnect. But at times they are overcome by striking transcendent affairs and disappear. All people are capable of putting larger issues before smaller ones, given the motivation, and can rise from lower, earthly borders to higher, spiritual ones.

Borders are greater problems among liberals and Romantics than among other types of people. Liberals and Romantics resist and fight against them. American poet Amy Lowell (1874-1925) summed up this attitude as well as one could in her effective poem "Patterns" when she cried "Christ! What are patterns for!" And American Revolutionary Tom Paine in *The Rights of Man* (1791-2) pointed out that one could break the patterns and borders imposed by man and events if one could begin society again from scratch. Literature provides an excellent field in which to examine borders and see how they impact on and control people's lives.

Crime fiction tends to be an excellent and useful literary prism through which to see many of the tensions in life, especially those having to do with conflict, with aggressiveness, with violence, with the cutting edge of people's behavior. Master mystery writer Ross Macdonald, himself a Canadian-American author, used detective fiction as a lightning rod revealing a culture's behavior. He wrote about Southern California because he felt that the geography and the resulting society created there were excellent case studies. To Macdonald, Southern California was the western border which Americans could not cross. There the westering urge of Americans had to come to a halt because it could not continue. The resulting cauldron of human activity, he felt, could be best analyzed in crime fiction. His studies, laced through with great understanding and compassion, demonstrate the value of such a field for study.

In different and freer ways, the American-Canadian border provides a similar laboratory model. This political border is looser and less congested, less culturally well-defined, but it is a strong political and cultural mark which both separates and joins the two cultures together. It is an object which is generally not noticed by most people until when stopped by the Customs people they are called upon to announce where they were born and where they have been. Yet it remains constantly in the back of the mind of most people who live within a two or three hundred mile proximity. The American continent north of Mexico actually consists of a bedding-down of similar people of two massive land-masses in a love-hate relationship, generally with compatibility but occasionally with domestic rows.

Four writers of Canadian detective fiction offer different approaches and developments of the border between the two sovereign states. One, perhaps the most significant of the four so far, is Howard Engel, who is studied in a separate paper in this collection. The other three offer three different studies. Two are rather casual in their use of the border; one uses it for profound reasons.

In *Murder by Microphone*, by John Reeves (New York: Avon, 1978), the references are only tangential. Since the story is one of murder in CBC-Radio one might think that there would be references to the media giants south of the border that blanket Canada with unwanted broadcasts, and which by law Canada has tried to keep out, at least through broadcasts over Canadian stations. But not so; the story is a witty presentation of Canadian life, and is a very tightly closed puzzle around the offices and personnel of the CBC. The only reference to anything American is a parallel of the arbitrary meanness of the murdered individual and the circumstances surrounding the American Watergate episode.

In *The Soda Crackers*, by Jaron Summers (Don Mills, Ont.: General Paperbacks, 1981) the political reference is a little more explicit. The story begins with a parade in Vancouver when a Governor of the state of Montana visits Vancouver for the "BC Sea Festival." Although this occasion triggers a series of crises, the hero of the story thinks that such public political events are "right." They are normal for Vancouver. Although the story has a great deal to do with drug running, and Vancouver is the drug capital of Canada, and there is occasion to talk about the drug trade in the sea and its relationship to U.S. there is no development.

Though the references in these two Canadian writers to the border are minimal and really are only reference points, and show a general unselfconscious autonomy of Canada, in the third study, *Dead in the Water*, by Ted Wood (Toronto: Seal Books, 1983), the development is much more complex in various kinds of borders and especially to the poltical demarcation between the United States and Canada.

Reid Bennett, chief of police of small up-province Murphy's Harbour, is a complicated individual with many borders to bother him. He has lines separating him from urban life in Toronto, from women (his wife left him after he returned from Vietnam and got into trouble), by honesty from the rest of corrupt society, by age from a group of outlaw bikers who taunt him and would like to beat him up. But by patience, good heart and care he manages to release the tensions compressed by these aspects of life. Forced by the Toronto Police Force to resign, rather than live in the city and become an object of ridicule by the media, he moves out into the country, to the small town of Murphy's Harbour, where he becomes Chief of Police, and learns to love the country; in fact, at the end of the book he turns down a job that would pay a good extra $10,000 a year with life in Toronto because he wants to test the small town life for a longer period before he recrosses the borders he was pushed over.

He recrosses the border of estrangement from women, caused by his wife's leaving him, by having what he calls "short stays" with various females; he resists temptation and does not conspire to run cocaine from his position, and he manages to release the tension between himself and the young bikers by playing the situation cool and giving them their rights as citizens. These are, in effect, the sensible and decent way to cross the borders that continually present themselves in life, that everybody has to deal with in one way or another.

But on a political and political-cultural level Ted Wood, the author of the book, through Reid Bennett, has a much greater and more real contact with the border separating the two nations Canada and the United States.

This effectively conceived and executed book is the first by Ted Wood, an English emigree to Canada in 1954. He worked on the Toronto police force for three years and subsequently wrote copy and served as agency creative director for an advertising firm in Toronto, before moving to a farm north of Toronto. He knows of the materials he writes about.

With his somewhat mixed background, his attitude toward Canada and the United States as revealed in Reid Bennett is not clear. Bennett is a man of violence—violence broke up his home and got him kicked off the Toronto police force; the only way he knew to handle people was to "put them down so they stay down." This is a trait that developed when he was serving in the U.S. Army in Vietnam. So he owes this streak of violence, and all it subsequently cost him, to the United States Army. But his attitude toward this episode in his life is ambivalent. Clearly the U.S. caused his fall from the normal life by teaching him violence. But he had volunteered for service in Vietnam. And he had done this at a time when American "guys were running to Canada to avoid" the draft and consequent service in Vietnam. In volunteering for this army service, Bennett had "broken faith with the liberals" who thereafter shunned him. So his contempt for the "liberals" of Canada shows through at the same time his respect for the American actions in Vietnam is clear. He did not regret his decision although the consequeneces were destroying him now.

But Bennett is under no illusions that only good emanates from the United States. The story covers a group of Americans who come to his small town of Murphy's Harbour and gradually get themselves and some Canadians to engage in illicit drug trafficking and subsequently killed off. Their presence in Canada is not unusual; hundreds of thousands of Americans spend the summer there. These, however, it gradually unfolds, are up to some kind of complicated and nefarious schemes. After some bodies have been found, Bennett begins to question Angela Masters, an American "kind of groupie," who has been connected with one of the disappeared men. She refuses to tell him much about her American and Canadian associates because she has been cautioned by her man friend not to say anything. Her taciturnity only leads to frustration on Bennett's part. One of the people who have been killed has been a Security Man from New York City, and Bennett is sent another from Bonded Securities to assist in solving the mystery. This one is from Toronto. His name is Simon Fulwell, and from his appearance we gather that Bennett is glad indeed not to have settled the border dispute with the Toronto police because the city is obviously not a place to make one look and be healthy. Fulwell is "a big man with an old-fashioned fedora flat on his head. He was about forty, good build, sallow complexion, pale blue eyes, hair sandy, dusting to gray at the temples. I thought: copper!" Though he starts out with questionable credentials, Fulwell is in fact a competent security man and detective, and assumes significant proportions in assisting Bennett solve the murders.

Fulwell, though working for the New York based Securities company, shares the usual feeling Canadians have about Americans, and that is not necessarily favorable. Americans always condescend to Canadians, he says: "New York. They still think they're the world and the rest of us are outer space" (p. 53). And it is this same feeling of superiority of Americans which keeps Angela Masters, the leading female associate of the murdered people, from telling Bennett—to her mind a rube cop—all that she knows about the individuals she is mixed up with.

In this novel, violence is violent, as it is in some of the other Canadian thriller fiction, especially *Soda Crackers*, and takes a strange turn in both of these novels. In both the guilty persons are interested in castrating the men. Undoubtedly this quirk has something to do with cutting off the procreative powers of the man and may be a Canadian reaction to the frontier spirit unleashed in America and which in the Canadian male clashes with urbanization.

Dead in the Water differs from most detective fiction in one of the main assistants the hero has. Bennett's assistant, along with the security agent sent up from Toronto, is a dog named Sam. He is well trained to follow directions and is better than two good armed men at putting desperate evil people down.

With or without Sam, there is plenty of what has come to be called regeneration through violence in this novel. The book proves that the border and the tensions between the two aspects of life can be lessened, profitably for the participants. By the end of the novel the British chemist who had synethesized cocaine and thus caused all the violence that occurred had recanted, felt guilty and straightened himself out. Fulwell, the replacement agent from Toronto who has come up to the woods looking pale and every ounce a jaded cop had developed into a new person who looked "spry. New suit, even a new hat" (p. 148). Angela Masters had recovered her human and admirable attributes. But the main beneficiary of all the action in the book is Bennett himself. Having been offered a job in Toronto at a sizeable increase in salary, Bennett has decided that he probably likes Murphy's Harbour after all and "wanted to see a whole year come and go in this place" (p. 151) before deciding if he would like to recross the border and go back into urban, commercial and "civilized" life. The border that had separated him from these aspects of life may have been his benefactor instead of his detractor.

At the end of the book, after having been offered opportunities to turn south, Bennett and Sam went out to see if they were smarter than the walleyes; they went fishing. They set out for the water. "He [Sam] trooped after me and I went out of the door and headed for home to pick up my fishing rod. I was surprised to find that I was whistling." Perhaps

Bennett had been purged of his violence, society had been gentled, and the Canadian-American border had disappeared because he no longer looked for it.

No doubt border fiction has different symbols and interpretations to people on different sides of the border. Canadian-American fiction often supplies what the reader is looking for. In crime fiction the reader must look carefully and closely, because often the point is mentioned tangentially or casually, yet is revealing. In Canadian detective fiction, we have already got a good picture in Wood's *Dead in the Water* and expect more in the future.

Wood's latest effort, *Live Bait* (1986), is something of a turnaround from the earlier novels, with a slight change in emphasis and a complete change in physical setting.

Unlike the earlier novels, this one begins in an action-intense setting in Toronto, with Reid Bennett, the Chief of Police in Murphy's Harbour, being attacked by two hoods swinging two-by-fours and trying to eliminate him. With the aid of his stand-by partner, Sam the police dog, Bennett is an over-match for the two hoods.

After this episode there is of course Wood's tie-in with Murphy's Harbour and an explanation of how Bennett happens to be in Toronto instead of back home tending store as he presumably should be. But he is actually on a two-week vacation, and had been invited to come to Toronto and assist a friend with some trouble he was having on construction sites.

Wood stays in Toronto for the entire novel, and Reid Bennett is engaged in a world that is much different from that in Murphy's Harbour. In Toronto, the plot is complicated and the action fast and dangerous. The construction that brings Bennett to Toronto in the first place is being interfered with by a mafia-like group based in Hong Kong and operating through a local branch. Their arms are long and their hands heavy. They have muscle and they have spies located in the highest places to be sure that the people they are blackmailing do not see and work with the wrong people.

Bennett's past continually influences his present attitude and behavior. He lets the readers know that he served in Vietnam with the U.S. Army. He also points out several times that in his past he once killed two people and their deaths shadow his existence. He also makes a big to-do over his Chinese wife who was killed while he was a witness. So the story surges with poignancy and grief.

But it also surges with immediacy. Bennett is almost caught because of the attractiveness of another Chinese lady, who admits that Westerners are bewitched by "exotic" ladies and capitalizes on her appearance. Bennett sees his former wife in this new look-alike and falls for her like a fool. She uses him both sexually and professionally. Caught in the web are various other people, including Bennett's sister and children in whose house he lives in Toronto.

Even more important in this novel than in the earlier ones is Sam, the police dog that is Bennett's strong right hand—and at times left too. Sam is the same remarkable dog he has been in the earlier novels—understanding virtually all kinds of commands—some with real subtlety—and acting them out with great virtuosity. When it comes to assistants, Sam is better than two men with guns.

In many ways this book is superior to the earlier ones, if the reader likes another example of a fine novel centered in an urban district rather than a rural one. Wood knows his Toronto as a veteran ex-police officer should. He writes extremely well. His language is idiomatic, powerful, explosive, snappy. Yet despite its power, this book somehow fails to maintain the individuality the earlier ones had because it has much more competition with its urban setting. Toronto could be Buffalo, New York, New York City, Chicago or any other American city. Murphy's Harbour is unique. At the end of the book, Bennett and Sam return to their small town to finish their vacation. They had made a lot of money in Toronto, but they wanted to enjoy it back in Murphy's Harbour. Perhaps Wood's efforts might benefit if he keeps Bennett working there.

But wherever he is located, Bennett will undoubtedly continue to be interested in humanity and will continue to fight not for himself but for the good of the community. In this novel he is in serious trouble and under normal circumstances might have taken flight back to the comparative security and safety of rural Canada. But there are two overwhelming forces at work. The first is, of course, a matter of pride and ego-involvement. Once Bennett gets into the conspiracy and sees evil trying to take over at least one portion of society, he is determined to stick in and bring his correction to evil to triumph. So he is determined not to be a loser. But overriding his personal involvement is the question of should Toronto and humankind be forced to submit to the evil embodied in this mafia-like organization and the scum employed as enforcers. The answer is obviously negative, and Bennett is therefore determined to see it through. After the evil has been flushed out of the social and human body he will give in, but not before.

This theme is nicely and completely worked out in this latest novel by Wood. The theme, and Wood's manner of working it out, gives the work a strength it could not otherwise have had.